MONEY DETOX

Dear Ruth,
you are enough!
Love, Tany

D1496256

MONEY DETOX

YOUR INVITATION TO LIBERATION

TAMMY LALLY
The Money Coach™

Little Lindsey Press

Money Detox

Your Invitation to Liberation

©2018 Tammy Lally, Maitland, Florida
First Printing August 2018
Little Lindsey Press
www.tammylally.com

ISBN: 978-0-692-15834-0

Cover design: Steven Michael Fies
Graphics: Kent D'Angelo
Headshot photo: Tamara Knight

Dedication

I dedicate this book to all who have taught me what I know—my clients, my friends, my family, my teachers, and the Divine.

I also include all of you who have experienced childhood trauma and have told yourself there is something wrong with you. There is nothing wrong with you. Bad things happened to you, and they have affected the hardwiring of your brain, making money and life all the more difficult. My intention is to bring you healing through understanding that you are not alone and money is not your worth.

With love and gratitude to my brother, Keith Patrick Lally, because without his story, mine may have never been told.

One hundred percent of the proceeds resulting from the sale of this book will be donated to Suicide Prevention.

Contents

Acknowledgements

Throughout the process of writing, I was touched again and again by the willingness of so many to give of themselves in the interest of helping this book come to life. I had many rumbles with God, and it has been a profound experience of faith, focus, shame, resilience, and love.

My heartfelt gratitude goes to the dozens of women whose unconditional love helped me see this book through.

To Marlayna Glynn for listening to my entire money detox and providing space for me to heal. Thank you for your devotion, generosity, and laborious work in helping me give voice, beauty, and validation to my most painful shameful stories.

To my first draft readers and teachers, Heather Kaye, Cindy Franklin, Brenda Samara, Deborah Price, Katherine Davidson, and Edwene Gaines; your love, enthusiasm, helpful feedback, and spiritual guidance allowed me to learn more, grow deeper, and release a lot of stories.

To my loving tribe, thank you for helping me rise stronger: Ire, Brennie, Jane, Katherine, Kanu, Kayla, Mom, Sarita, Judy, June, Claudine, Kathy, Terri, Patty, Lynette, Jennifer, Jessie, Vera, Kari, Lori, Pamela, Carolann, Amy, Phyllis, Donna, Cathleen, Angel, Suman, Kim, Rita Ray, and Pat.

What follows is a true story that is based on my experiences and perceptions. I share this in love and hope for healing. Most of the names and personal characteristics of the individuals involved have been changed in order to disguise their identities.

Introduction

Any situation that teaches us greater humility, sobriety, wisdom about self and others, responsibility, forgiveness, depth of reflection, better decision making, and what's truly important is not an ultimate failure.

— Marianne Williamson

Have you come from a difficult or painful family background? You may be surprised to learn a dysfunctional family's emotional legacy often becomes the foundation for an adult addictive personality, which in turn often manifests as financial stress.[1] This book is a unique guide for you to recognize and resolve old emotional wounds that are keeping you from living the life you were born to live. You will find within these pages a way to heal childhood trauma by recognizing you are not what you inherited, you are not what has happened to you. It is my sincere hope that

---

1. Deane Alban, "12 Effects of Chronic Stress on Your Brain," *Be Brain Fit* (January 21, 2018), bebrainfit.com/effects-chronic-stress-brain/.

this book will help you liberate yourself from debilitating addictions, restore yourself to wholeness, and rewrite your story.

Chances are if you've picked up this book, you've experienced money stress. If you dig deep into your psyche, you will probably discover a well of *money shame*. One of the most powerful ways to heal money shame is to go through what I call a *money detox*.

So what is money shame, you ask? And why would I think you have it when I don't even know you?

While working with thousands of clients over my seventeen years in the financial industry, I couldn't help but notice an undeniable and alarming pattern. All of my clients had financial fear (which is no surprise since I am a money coach), but it became apparent to me that all of their money fears were one symptom of a single and more significant issue: money shame—that is, feelings of guilt, embarrassment, and humiliation tied to their finances. Naturally, I became curious about how money shame develops. I noticed that the stories I heard in my office followed a pattern, regardless of the individual details. I call it the *circle of money pain*

- Inherited money beliefs

- Emotional pain and trauma

- Resentments

- Lack of forgiveness
- Need to relieve pain
- Self-harm through money

I soon realized these patterns play out not only for individuals but also on a bigger scale within our society. Money is perennially among the leading sources of stress, according to the APA's *Stress in America* survey.[2] Financial stress is a contributing factor in conflict in relationships, divorce, addiction, illness, and suicide. As reported by Princeton researchers Anne Case and Angus Deaton, financial stress is a likely factor in the rising rates of mortality, including by suicide, among white middle-aged men,[3] a statistic that has affected my family and me firsthand—a story I will share with you in the following pages.

But you don't need me to point out the effects of financial stress. You can see it all around you. You can read the daily stories in the news about how we are jumping off buildings and bridges, putting guns in our mouths, and shooting up the office to escape the deadly circle of money shame, stress, and fear.

2. American Psychological Association, *Stress in America: The State of our Nation* (November 1, 2017), http://www.apa.org/news/press/releases/stress/2017/state-nation.pdf.
3. Anne Case and Angus Deaton, "Rising Morbidity and Mortality in Midlife Among White Non-Hispanic Americans in the 21st Century," *PNAS* 112, no. 49 (December 8, 2015): 15078-83.

Contrary to popular belief, financial stress is not the private domain of the poor. Not by a long shot. If you think money shame doesn't cross the poverty line, then think again. Money shame is an equal-opportunity condition; we can all experience it, regardless of gender, financial status, faith, neighborhood, city, or race. My clients range from millionaires who worry about mismanaging or losing what they already have, to working-class folks buried in debt, to those who can't figure out how to keep the lights on. Some of my clients are individuals. Some are couples, and some are families with children. Some clients are the leaders of organizations who have recognized that money shame can cause a debilitating trickle-down effect on their employees, volunteers, patients, and clients. Despite the wide variance in bank balances, money shame is a problem that is more common than you might realize.

After working with clients who represent nearly every distinct type of financial scenario you could imagine, I couldn't help but begin asking questions:

- Why do all my clients share one common factor: shame?

- What exactly is money shame?

- How does it cause financial stress?

- Why do people end up in debt?

- Why do relationships fall apart?

- Why are so many addicted to shopping, alcohol, drugs, sex, and other numbing habits?

I did not have to look far for the answers. I talk to people about money every day. So it was apparent to me that shame was the #1 emotion that comes up for people. I was determined to get to the root of this insanity called money shame. In addition, I sought to identify how the problem developed, so I could reach potential clients before they needed my help.

To speak about money shame, I had to break the rules—the long-established family rules of secrecy, shame, and perfection. I had to reveal the truth about how running marathons on the financial treadmill to keep up with the Joneses nearly wiped out my family. Sadly, not all of us survived. But I did, and I am here to tell our stories, and to share with you the process I developed, which I call the *money detox*.

Writing a book, going public with all of my money shame shenanigans, allowed me to delve into another layer of detox and healing. I have stepped deeper into my authentic power during the process. I have looked more closely at my numbing behaviors. For example, I stopped beating up my body in boot-camp workouts and instead practice yoga daily. I put down sugar and gluten after years of health issues from overconsumption. I no longer shop as a sport; I buy what I need. Change is not always immediately. I've found addressing one numbing habit at a time to be enough. I also recommend lots of self-love and patience.

The money detox is a transformative process that happens through embracing the seven elements of healing. It begins when you release your money stories. Unpacking and healing your childhood money trauma allows you to move from a space of "there is something wrong with me" to a space of "something happened to me and I'm learning from it and dealing with it." The result of a money detox is true liberation and financial freedom.

In this book, for the first time, I describe the money detox process as a series of seven elements of healing that build upon each other to lead you toward financial freedom. When I say "financial freedom," I don't just mean having more money in your pocket; I'm talking about a psychological and spiritual revolution that can free you from the inner forces that perpetuate money problems in your life. Each element in the process includes exercises you can do either on your own or with a partner. I also include stories and anecdotes in each chapter. I have learned and healed so much through working with my clients. I want to give what I learned back to you.

The money detox draws on some of the valuable tools I learned through The Money Coaching Institute, which I use regularly with clients and which I have blended over the years with my own knowledge and wisdom. I received my coach training and certification from the Institute, which trains coaches and financial advisers by combining psychological and spiritual principles with practical financial guidance to help clients identify and change their core money beliefs. Here, I draw on those principles with the blessings of the Institute's founder, Deborah Price.

I encourage and support you to engage in the seven elements of the money detox process. While learning about the money detox, listen to yourself, start a money journal, write down all your discoveries (big and small), stay curious about yourself, and take on new practices you can do daily. We become what we practice. We become what we commit to change. Along the way, be kind to yourself. Understand that you will break a practice; just forgive yourself and recommit. As you follow the money detox process, you will discover that it has the power to change everything for you.

1

Own Your Money Story

You either wall inside your story and own it, or you stand outside your story and hustle for your worthiness.

— Brené Brown

My own story begins with my older brother Keith. On his fortieth birthday in 2007, he called me. I could hear the embarrassment in his voice: "Tam, I'm in dire straits. I would not ask unless I had to, but can I borrow $7,500?"

It was not the first time I had received a call from him of this nature. I had been helping Keith and his family for a while. This time, however, the tone of his voice alarmed me. I had never heard him sound so beaten down, so sick, so hopeless. Naturally, I agreed to help. I would loan him the money immediately, under the condition that I meet with him and his wife, Karen, to discuss what was going on with their finances. Why were they always behind? Why was it they never seemed to catch up?

Since I was the financial professional in the family (and I was willing to loan him the money), Keith readily agreed to my terms. We met at a Starbucks. I came prepared, wearing my financial planner game face and ready to spout my newly brewed tough-love script. I began with the math questions:

"How much do you make?"

"Where is the money going?"

"Where can you cut back on expenses?"

"How can you increase your income?"

After a quick review of the math and their credit reports, I offered my sound advice, sure to point my finger and use a firm tone of voice: "You should both get new, higher-paying jobs. You should work more hours. You should sell your toys. You should sell your home. You should take the kids out of private school. You should cut back on Starbucks. You should stop shopping. You should stop drinking alcohol. You should stop smoking cigarettes. You should sell some hunting rifles. You should stop taking expensive vacations."

In other words, *shame on you, shame on you, shame on you,* ad nauseam.

My brother and his wife immediately devolved into a fearsome blame game with each other.

"It's your fault."

"You did this!"

"If only you would..."

"If only you wouldn't..."

I vacillated between therapist, referee, financial professional, and pissed-off sister. I wanted them both to be "better"—to act responsibly, to think about the impact of their actions, to grow the hell up. They were no longer the footloose, fancy-free, hard-partying high school sweethearts they'd once been. They were the parents of two children now. With their adult lives came adult responsibilities that, to me, they still didn't seem to grasp.

Their lives were so much messier than I knew, yet I was a dog with a bone: I kept circling back around to the mathematical solutions. By the end of our five-hour-plus meeting, we were all emotionally exhausted (and I am sure the Starbucks staff was, too). We called it quits, hugged, and kissed goodbye. I felt a bit smug as I drove away in my S-Class Mercedes. I would have patted myself on the back if I'd been able to reach. After all, I'd given my brother and his wife the best financial advice I could give under the circumstances: make more and spend less.

On the drive home, totally oblivious to the truckload of shame I had just dumped on them, I called our mother to tell her about the meeting.

But Keith had reached her first. "Tammy wasn't helpful," he'd said. He felt beaten up, hurt, and alone. "I don't have anyone to turn to. There's no one on my side, Mom." Rather than feel hopeful with all that darn good advice I'd shoved his way, he'd turned to hopelessness instead.

I immediately called him, but he didn't pick up the phone. I felt brokenhearted, misunderstood, and so despondent. I had the greatest of intentions when I met with my brother and his wife. I wanted to "fix" them and their situation. But my efforts had fallen far from the intended mark. I tried to call Keith many times over the following month to talk through our misunderstanding, but we never connected.

Set Aside Your Ideas About Money

Money is the source of pain for so many people. Whether you call it money, finances, or wealth, you have a whole set of money beliefs. Of course, these beliefs are different for everybody. Some believe money is unattainable. Some believe they have an overwhelming responsibility to manage it properly. Some believe they don't have enough. Some belief they have too much. Some belief money is the root of all evil. But everybody identifies in some way with money. We all deal with it; we all need it. For virtually all of us, money is an inevitable part of living life on this planet.

In my coaching practice, I start by asking if clients are willing to set aside their preexisting thoughts, ideas, and emotional baggage about money. Likewise, I ask you now if you are willing to put your money thoughts and beliefs on a shelf, or in a closet, or in a box, and leave them there as you come with me on this journey. I want you to start anew, with a clean slate, to allow yourself to be open to the concepts and thoughts and perspectives I am going to share with you.

More than likely, you come with damaged belief systems about money that have to be set aside before you can truly change and grow. How do I know this? Because I used to be there. Because I see the patterns daily in my practice. You wouldn't be having the financial experiences you're having if your beliefs were grounded in love and faith in a higher power. Love and faith give you the willingness to abandon the story you've been carrying around all your life about yourself and money—a story you most likely have not yet fully articulated to yourself, let alone to anyone else. I'm asking you to shelve your money beliefs so you can make space to hear and heal your own story.

But first, let me continue a bit further with my own story.

The Unthinkable

On April 28, 2007, about two months after my Starbucks meeting with Keith, I awoke from a deliciously deep sleep as the airplane wheels were unfolding to meet the runway in Miami. I was returning from a pilgrimage to Peru I had gone on with my girlfriend, Tara, and a few of her friends.

The primary purpose of the trip was to visit Tara's spiritual teacher, Nazario, the caretaker for his people high in the mountains. We'd been due back on April 27, but had missed our connection in Lima due to poor weather. Now we were all feeling worn out and anxious to get home.

Tara and I had been dating for about a year and a half. She happened to be wealthy. On that trip, I had been witness to a side of her I hadn't seen before and that I didn't like. Constantly in such close quarters, I found myself growing increasingly uncomfortable around her. She had a perfectionist standard that no one else seemed capable of meeting. Nothing was good enough for her. She complained a lot, and I began to experience her as negative, in general, and ungrateful for all she had.

Outwardly, I was silent about my thoughts. But I was internally raging: *Are you kidding me? You've got all this money, and you're miserable? You can do whatever you want! You don't even have to work! Why are you so cranky all the time? You're wealthy, for God's sake! Get grateful, lady!* And it wasn't just Tara. Her friends were also wealthy. I was a working woman—not living paycheck to paycheck, but a worker bee nonetheless. I had to earn my standard of living, while these women had received inheritances through birth or marriage. I felt like an outsider, which created a sense of not belonging, despite the beauty of Peru and her people.

When I met privately with Nazario for a coca leaf reading, he said the person I was with wasn't right for me.

He recommended I move on. Because I had already been exploring that line of thinking myself, I trusted his judgment and ended my relationship with Tara in the midst of the trip. This eased my feelings of not belonging in the short term, but the grief soon became overwhelming. I had a big dream with Tara, one which was deeply rooted in my money story.

After our plane landed, I began listening to my voicemail messages. There was one from a childhood friend, Cathy, who urged me to call her right away. Cathy and I talked only once a year, unless there was a birth, divorce, or death, so I was curious why she had called. But she didn't leave her number, and I didn't know it offhand.

Tara was also checking her own messages. When she looked up, I mentioned that Cathy had called. "Someone must have died," I said off-the-cuff, "because she rarely calls."

Tara suggested waiting until we got through customs to phone anyone. "Miami on a Saturday night, Tam? Think of the lines!"

That made sense to me, so we de-boarded and went off to get our bags, say our goodbyes, and head to our separate connecting gates. I had a two-hour layover, so I was moving quickly, ahead of the others, hoping to catch an earlier flight to North Florida, where I lived. Besides, the phone call from Cathy was niggling at me. Perhaps something had happened to her mom or brother? I decided to give my mom a call as soon as I got to the baggage claim area to make sure everything was okay.

I was waiting at the elevator for the others to catch up with me, when Tara's friend Elizabeth came around the corner. She looked sad. Almost in a whisper, she said, "Tammy, Tammy, Tammy. Life can be so hard."

That seemed a bit maudlin, so I put my hand on her shoulder and asked if she was okay. She didn't respond.

Tara was right behind her, and the three of us walked into the elevator together. As I turned around, Tara looked me in the eyes, and without preamble, said, "I have bad news. Jane left me a message saying your brother Keith committed suicide last night."

It was just like that. No warm-up. No prelude. The delivery was so unexpected, it shocked me to my core. The door whisked shut, turning the tiny elevator into what felt like a cage with all the air sucked out. It felt as if someone or something was pressing so hard against my chest I couldn't take a breath. The room began to spin around me, and I grabbed hold of Tara's arm to keep from falling to the floor in a faint. A tide of panic washed over my body, and in its wake, I couldn't control any aspect of myself. I started pacing. I began to cry, to hiccough, to talk, to interrupt myself. I was out of control, while trying to remain in control at the same time.

The reality was just too much for my mind. I was in no state to be in public. All I wanted to do was hide out in a little private space until I could get on my connecting flight. As I holed up in the quietest corner I could find near my scheduled departure gate, Tara did her best to find an earlier flight for me.

I called my family and learned the horrifying details: Keith had shot himself in the chest with a crossbow, while his little girl was playing outside and his wife was in the other room. He had bled out and died by the time the ambulance reached the hospital.

There is just no way to prepare yourself for a reality of that nature about someone you love. My childhood best friend; my sidekick; my beautiful, lovable, older brother was gone from the Earth. I had never known a day when Keith wasn't there. His death—his self-inflicted death—was an impossible thought.

Eventually, Tara prevailed in finding me a seat on an earlier flight, and I was Northern Florida bound. As soon as I boarded my flight, the first thing I did was order two glasses of wine and down them in quick succession.

On the way home, I realized Keith had taken his life on April 27—the day I would have been home had our flight from Peru not been delayed. My thoughts raced through what I could have done if I had been there. Would that have changed anything? Would it, really?

See, we had a long-established pattern, Keith and I:

- He would get into a fight with his wife, Karen.

- Karen would call me and say, "Your brother's talking crazy."

- I would get on the phone with him, and he would tell me stories about her in return.

- Next, I would ask what was going on with his drinking.

- He would agree to go to detox.

- I would press him to agree to continue treatment after detox, but he would say he couldn't afford it.

- I would say, "I'll pay for it."

- He would go into detox.

- I would press him to go into treatment.

- He would say he couldn't go into treatment because he had to go back to work for the money.

- I would repeat, "I'll pay for your treatment."

- He would say he couldn't take time off because he needed the money.

- I would say, "You're gonna be dead, man! Forget about the money. You're gonna be dead."

As it turned out, I had been right. Now Keith was dead. Just as I'd feared.

I was devastated, riddled with quilt, shame, and remorse. Our last conversation had been me shaming him. Oh my God, the power of words: *Had I shamed him to death?* How could I live with this? I felt broken beyond repair.

How did this happen?

Looking back at our Starbucks meeting, my brother didn't need a financial plan. What he needed was a breakthrough from his suffering. He needed compassion.

Keith was not going to be the one in our family to break the mold, as he'd hoped to do, so I was left behind to do the job.

Aftershocks and Heartbreak

My world was breaking and cracking, and I continued to feel the aftershocks throughout Keith's funeral and beyond.

I arrived at my brother's home in the early evening. No one wanted to believe Keith had killed himself. There was too much shame, too much reality, too much pain in that line of thinking. The buzz in the house was "Why? Why? Why?" We were all in shock, looking around for whom to blame and whom to shame.

As I entered what we knew as Keith's office—actually, the garage—I sensed his presence. With a bittersweet smile, I thought, *Of course he's here. Where else would he be?* Despite his struggles, Keith had always been devoted to his family, and I felt sure he would want to make certain we were okay. Although I wouldn't say any of us could even remotely be considered okay at that moment.

In Keith's office, I found the plain and simple truth. He did not leave a note, at least not a formal one. He didn't have to, as the evidence of his despair was staggering and inarguable:

- Eight cases of empty beer bottles
- Empty pain medication containers
- Ashcans full of cigarette butts
- A stack of unpaid, delinquent bills
- A foreclosure notice on his home, delivered the day of his death
- A paystub that just wasn't enough

The following day, Tara accompanied me to the private family viewing for Keith. During the drive to the funeral parlor, Karen called me in hysterics. My oldest and estranged brother, James, had shown up for the viewing and had brought along his wife, Teresa. Sounds reasonable, right? Not in my family. James and Keith hadn't spoken for four years. James had missed years of his younger brother's life. Now Karen didn't want him there.

I made a failed attempt to calm Karen. "Just relax. I'll talk to James, and we will figure it all out when I get there."

The parking lot was already full of family members and close friends when we arrived. I found James and Teresa sucking on cigarettes in front of the funeral parlor door. My approach was cautious and calculated. First, I offered them consoling hugs and made some niceties. Then I asked the question that changed the family dynamic for years to come: "James, would you mind asking Teresa to stay in the visitors' area and let Karen go in to see Keith first?"

James exploded. "No way! She killed my brother! Fuck her! She's responsible for his death. Keith is *my* brother!" Then he burst into tears.

Despite his breakdown, or perhaps because of it, I was able to steer him away from the parlor, while the women moved swiftly inside. James tore himself from my arms and ran off to the parking lot to join some like-minded friends of the family. They kicked off an alcohol-fueled tailgating party to console themselves.

I joined my mom and Marie to view Keith's body. I was seeing him for the first time since that Starbucks meeting, and the guilt and questions were eating me alive. In contrast, the room was peaceful and quiet. Pictures of Keith were displayed behind the casket. He had been a baseball player in his youth, and I looked upon him in his uniform with a tremendous feeling of loss and regret. He was so beautiful and happy, and my stomach twisted as I faced how long it had been since he'd looked that way. Years. A decade. Maybe two. There were no pictures from his later years. It was painful to come face to face with his journey into despair. How had we not noticed? Why hadn't we done more during the limited time we had together?

The three of us knelt together before the casket. Mom reached out to touch her son's hair and skin for the last time. Marie looked down at her daddy's face in utter shock. We had a mere ten minutes of quiet reflection, when really what we needed was hours, days, weeks, months, and years. I began an internal conversation with Keith, trusting that wherever he was, he could hear me: *I know you suffered. I hope you are now free of the pain. I understand how you were hurting. I love you, my brother.*

I heard a sudden scuffling as Alisha, Karen's mother, raced into the room on fast feet. Alisha was in her seventies, a petite woman of Asian descent. A screech erupted from her as she strode toward Keith, beginning a death wail that seemed much too large to come from her small frame. Before my shocked eyes, her trim, elf-like body, with gymnast's legs, climbed the side of the casket and landed on top of my brother—her beloved son-in-law. She straddled his body as she wailed to the heavens.

My reaction was utter astonishment. I nervously burst into a giggle as a strange combination of mortification, shock, and surprise washed over me. I could only whisper, *Keith, I get it. There's just too much drama to live through.*

I did get it. For the first time, I saw with full clarity the extent of the insanity around me, and I knew I could choose not to embrace it. I wasn't stuck with it. I didn't have to try to fix it.

Mental illness.

Alcoholism.

Codependency.

Shame.

Powerlessness.

As Alisha rocked Keith's casket back and forth, I was hit with a lightning bolt of clarity: I had to make changes. But first I had to get Alisha out of the casket. So I set off to find my mother.

Upon hearing the news, my mother turned frantic, ever the protector of family shame. "If Alisha knocks the casket over, Keith's shirt will fall off, and Marie will see the patch covering the hole," she said. "Hurry! Go get the guys in the parking lot to get Alisha off his body."

I interrupted James as he was slugging down a beer. "Whaddya want, troublemaker?" he said.

Ignoring the barb, I said, "We've got problems. Alisha is in Keith's casket."

James laughed so hard he spit out his beer on the asphalt at his feet. The other guys followed suit. Honestly, it was hard to believe how the chaos was unfolding.

"We have to get her out of there before he falls out and Marie sees the hole in his chest," I urged. "Come on! Now!"

It took four grown men to peel tiny Alisha's legs and arms from Keith's corpse and get her out of the casket.

In the days following the funeral, we learned Keith had left behind no life insurance. We searched his home for a policy, certain he would have provided for his wife and children in the event of his death. Surely he hadn't taken his life, knowing he'd left no money behind to cover his loss? But we were met with devastation. His policy had lapsed from nonpayment. When he tried to renew the policy, he no longer qualified due to the many years he had abused his body. He had failed the medical exam. Likely, he felt ashamed and therefore didn't share this turn of events with anyone.

Karen had believed Keith had a half-million dollar policy in place. When she learned the truth, that he had taken his life without providing for her and their children, her recriminations began anew. *How could he leave us like this? How did he think we would survive?* Probably not unlike many others, after taking in the shock of her husband's death, it was money that took precedence in her mind.

Despite the funeral drama, my family jumped in to raise funds for Karen and the kids. We got the house out of foreclosure and made sure Karen was financially stable. The money raised was set up in a fund for the children's education, as well as an emotional support fund. However, Karen fell back into destructive money patterns, mishandling most of the money on pizza parties for the neighborhood kids, along with shopping and dining out. Not long after, the home we had tried to save went into foreclosure once again. This was yet another heartbreak.

Breaking the Cycle

Life has myriad ways to get our attention. You might feel a gentle tap on your shoulder. You might hear a quiet whisper in your ear, telling you that perhaps you ought to think about changing course. Or it could be a push in the middle of your back. Well, in my case, it took a two-by-four over the head to get my attention. Keith's death was that block of wood over the head, delivered with such force I could no longer deny the reality of my surroundings. The fact that I went straight from the spiritual peace of Peru and the comfortable, wealthy world of Tara and her friends to the addicted maelstrom of my family only heightened the impact.

Keith's death ripped the blinders from my eyes. It set me on a path I didn't anticipate or understand at the time. I finally began to make the connection between my family legacy of pain and suffering and its impact on my mental, emotional, and financial well-being. The stigma of family addictions, shame and sickness hit me with a force akin to a spiritual experience. Facing my family's many illnesses scared me straight, forcing me to surrender and to get help.

Before Keith's death, my Dalmatian, Lucy, had slept on

the floor beside my bed for the nine years she'd been with me. After his death, she made her way onto my bed. She slept this way for months, as if trying to protect me from the waves of grief that shook me. I knew that if I didn't make some changes, I was going to turn out just like the family from which I'd failed to distance myself.

At first, as I embarked on my journey to break the cycle, I was terrified to own my money story. It carried too much secrecy, silence, and shame. If I owned my story, I would have to admit that I was acting out of all my dysfunctional beliefs. I would have to begin by speaking up against my mother. That was too big for me, at least in the beginning. I'd had four decades of behaving in a way that kept her pacified. That was a hard one to break.

I started by identifying my biggest fear, which was the question of who would love me once I spoke up. *Would I be all alone, with no family?* I had to get to the place where I was okay with that. If that's what it took, I was willing.

But as I proceeded, I discovered our family and personal histories don't have to be the predictor of our futures.

It only takes one person to break the cycle.

I invite you to be that one in your family.

I invite you to be liberated from the power your money story has over you.

During this process, You can come to know why you are here, your purpose, your calling, your passion. You may become so inspired that you'll find a way to make money doing it.

Money shame is a silent killer that drives many of us to keep up with the Joneses. It creates a "rescue fantasy" state of mind, making it nearly impossible to break free. I said "nearly." You can break free from the grip of money shame by going on a money detox. As I have learned, once you see the truth about yourself, you cannot un-see it. No matter how far you may stray from it, it will always be calling you home. I hope the process described in this book will awaken you to your soul's call for healing, which will keep bringing you home, no matter how far you stray.

The way through it all involves a money detox: a gentle process of letting go of your money stories (real, imagined, brainwashed to believe, or inherited), heartbreaks, unrealized dreams, grievances, and money shame. This letting go can lead to knowing real wealth and emotional, psychological, and spiritual wellness. The only requirement for you is to have the courage, honesty, openness, and willingness to change. Transformation occurs when your entire being is addressed; for this reason, the money detox involves your whole being.

The seven elements of the money detox address the many ways we get trapped in harmful money patterns. These elements define a continuous flow of healing that you can move in and out of. It is not a linear process. You can enter at any point. The basic flow goes like this:

Element 1: Own your money story

Element 2: Recognize your spiritual crisis

Element 3: Uncover your shame

Element 4: Identify your money beliefs

Element 5: Discover your worth

Element 6: Make forgiveness a daily practice

Element 7: Live from a circle of money blessings

As you break down one element, you must deal with all the pain residue surrounding it. For example, if you overcome resentment but hang onto self-criticism, your self-criticism will pull you back into resentment. You may need a coach to help with that. Use the momentum you gain while working on one element to carry you on to the next element. As you do this, you will begin to see that you can relate to money from a more balanced state of being. You may stop overspending, underspending, or being obsessed with money. You will acquire a feeling of greater satisfaction, of feeling you have enough. You will begin to step out of the circle of money pain and into the circle of money blessings.

Your Money Story

I am a money coach today because I came to understand that money and shame about money are the central reasons many people get sick and addicted, take their lives, or leave their husbands or wives or families. As I will describe in more detail in the next chapter, my father left his wife and three children because he didn't want the responsibility of making money and paying financially for our support. Because of the demands of money, he never came back. I was left grieving the loss of a dream. As a money coach, I see day in and day out that I am not alone in this.

My first grievances were the loss of the family I wanted, the loss of the parents I wanted, the loss of the brothers I had. That was followed by realizing I had some emotional disorders to deal with, including anxiety, alcoholism, and codependency. I found myself grieving the loss of every relationship I'd ever had. I had to be willing to learn to grieve because that's a big part of what people don't want to feel, especially around money.

It has taken me years to chip away at my family's legacy of secrecy, shame, and cover-up. In my family—maybe much like yours—all of our dysfunction was related to money and shame, which made it even harder to recognize that we needed help. Why was it much harder? Because it's so taboo in our culture to discuss money. We suffer silently. We remain mum. We avoid having the conversations about money that we need to have. We are too ashamed to speak up. The reasons for feeling ashamed are many, and we will delve into those reasons in subsequent chapters.

We use debt and credit to feel better and to mask our grief. We buy houses we can't afford. We buy cars we can't afford. We send our kids to schools we can't afford. But we do all of these things because they are attached to our dream.

What happens when you're willing to admit it's all not true, that the dream you've been clinging to is not real? That is the jumping-off point. That's the point where, if you want to get to the truth, you have to be willing to look at the story you've told yourself. You have to be willing to peel back all the layers and find the truth in it all. Your willingness to examine must be unceasing. Each day, you must become ready to start over. You must have the desire to walk through whatever the day brings and not hide from reality. I know it's hard! But you are worth it.

I have just shared with you an important piece of my money story. Perhaps you found it distressing to read at points. Perhaps you thought I went into too much unpleasant detail. Or maybe my story touched you in a place of deep recognition. Either way, the reason I continue to share my story is so I can fully own it. I have come to understand through my experience, as well as that of many others with money problems, that owning our stories is the first element in the healing process.

We can't be successful on this journey alone. I tried. Part of the reason we get stuck is that we need at least one person we can share our story with. Life tends to give us a series of wake-up calls, yet we are too quick to hit the snooze button. I got a huge wake-up call, and I couldn't ignore it. My beloved brother had to die for me to face my fears. Sooner or later, you must wake up. Start by owning your story.

In this chapter, I talked about Keith's suicide because it was a breakthrough moment for me. It turned everything inside out and forced me to begin the process of change. Many of us can point to pivotal events, but that doesn't alter the fact that our stories begin early in life. So this first element is about doing the work, about going back and unearthing those crucial early stories, and then following them up through to the present day.

If you are familiar with the 12 steps of Alcoholics Anonymous, you will recognize the importance of admitting that we are powerless and that our life is unmanageable. That's what I meant when I spoke about being willing to ask for help. Part of asking for help is admitting our problem to God (or a higher power), to ourselves, and to another human being. That's why I ask you in the exercise at the end of this chapter to tell your story to one other person.

I realize it isn't easy to find safe people with whom to share our money stories. We are vulnerable to begin with, and shame increases our vulnerability. For this reason, you may choose to see a coach or therapist or healer—someone who understands what you are going through and can make you feel seen and heard. You don't have to see a professional to do this exercise (or any of the exercises in the book). If you don't know someone you feel safe sharing your story with, you can write it down in a journal and share it with a higher power.

In fact, whether or not you have someone to talk to, I strongly recommend you create a money journal in which you write down your story. You can start writing it down before you tell it to one other person. Or you can write it down afterwards. I can guarantee your story won't come to you all at once. You'll be driving along, and all of a sudden, a memory will pop up. You'll wake up from a dream and remember something else. An old photo will jog your memory. As your story comes back to you, use your money journal to keep track of all the pieces.

When I began my own money detox, I made a practice of sitting quietly, praying, and writing on a daily basis. I found prayer to be extremely helpful to un-stuff all my money memories. Sometimes I would feel overwhelmed and take a week or two off before I could come back to it. At other times, I would relapse and eat sugar or go shopping. I'd overspend. There was always some relapse behavior waiting to grab me. You can't count on the money detox process to be a straight route, as the crow flies. There are usually detours along the way. But I always found my way back to the process, and my journal was the one touchstone that kept me coming back.

Each chapter in this book ends with an exercise that relates to one or more of the seven elements of the money detox process. You can write your responses to these exercises in your money journal. The process of recording your responses will help you become clear about your own story and gain valuable insights about yourself.

SELF-DIRECTION #1: Tell Your Story

The first step of this exercise is best done with you and your higher power. Begin by sitting with your money journal and asking your God for help. For example, "God, Spirit, Universe, my past is blocking me from the sunlight of the spirit. Show me the truth about myself. Write through me. Let me be your secretary."

You have now primed the pump. Ask one question at a time. Write everything that comes forward, with no editing. I know this might sting. But you are worth it. Take your time, breathe. There's no rush. If it feels too overwhelming, take a break and come back to it.

Find one person you trust and tell him or her your truth. Don't judge yourself or your story. Use the following questions to guide your story:

1. What is my earliest memory of money?
Example: I remember my brother stealing my toys and forcing me to buy them back from him for twenty-five cents.

2. How did this experience make you feel?
Example: angry and sad. My brother was mean and manipulating with money. I grew up fearing him. To this day, I don't like him. He is cheap, a penny pincher.

3. How did the experience shape your money beliefs?
Example: I don't care about money and avoid dealing with it.

4. How do you treat your money?
Example: I give a lot of money away to charity.

It is normal if you don't recall much. Money pain and shame cause us to armor up. You may need a few tries to unlock your memories. Be gentle, be kind, and stay curious. Your memories will come forward when you are ready.

As you proceed, notice if you can see how one childhood experience with money shaped your present circumstances with money. As you continue, here are some additional questions to ask yourself:

- What happened around money when I was a child? A teenager?

- How was money talked about at home by my parents and siblings?

- How was money treated at home by my parents and siblings?

- How did I feel around money? (proud, anxious, fearful, don't recall)

- How did my parents react around money? (excited, respectful, fearful, braggadocios)

2

Recognize Your Spiritual Crisis

The reason I've been able to be so financially successful is my focus has never, ever for one minute been money.

— Oprah Winfrey

After Keith died, I stayed drunk for three weeks. Numbing myself was the only way I knew how to cope with that tremendous pain. Tara and I were on the splits after having broken up in Peru, so I weathered that terrible time on my own. I thought if I could drink enough alcohol, I might find some level of peace. Instead, I drank myself sober. My mind cleared briefly, and the thought appeared: *Go back to AA or you're going to die. You're going to go out the way Keith went out.*

Something inside me knew I was in spiritual crisis.

Except I didn't know it consciously in that moment. I

had taken a six-year break from AA after eleven years of sobriety. I thought I was cured of alcoholism and could drink like normal people. I'd even gone to see my therapist before I picked up my first drink. Now all that had flown out the window.

When I walked back into AA the third week after Keith's death, I stepped in as a victim of alcoholism. I'd learned early on from my mother how to do that: I was always the victim of someone or something else. So wearing that familiar persona, I walked into a meeting one Saturday morning. The room was full of old-timers. Only the spiritually fit would show up at 7 a.m. on a Saturday during Memorial Day weekend.

The gist of my sharing was "Poor me! Look what alcohol has done to me!" I thought people would ask how they could help me. I was ready to be rescued.

That was not what happened.

Once I finished my tale of woe, a woman stood up on the other side of the room and said in a great British accent, "Work the steps!" She pointed to the placard where the steps were listed for all to see and promptly sat back down.

It took me four months to hear her words. She eventually became a dear friend, and I have to say she played a part in saving my life. I saw her every day in meetings for years and years, and her wake-up call to me became an intrinsic part of my story, as well as what I recommend to clients and in this book.

I'm not saying it was all a smooth road. It was full of potholes and icy patches, and every obstacle or slowdown you could imagine. Sometimes it felt like I went through sponsors like they were yesterday's mail. Nevertheless, I believe we pick the people we need at the time we need them to help us through to the next level of consciousness. Sometimes we grow and change faster than our sponsors, mentors, spouses, partners, coaches, therapist, and friends can keep up with. And it's all okay. I believe this is part of how God graciously brings the right people at the right time to help us grow and wake up on the path.

I always wanted a magic solution to everything. For example, "I'll just say this prayer, and I'll be forgiven." Or "I'll just apologize, and I'll be forgiven." "I'll change my behavior, and they'll see I'm different." Or I'd pray for a bag of money to show up or winning lottery numbers.

Well, it doesn't happen that way. It has taken me years of walking this journey, and every single day I've had to engage in deep, thorough self-inquiry about my behavior. I had to look at all my dishonest thinking. All my selfish actions. All my self-seeking behaviors. All my resentments, and there were many. I had to look at myself from every aspect of relationship, sex, money—primarily sex and money, as those were the two major areas I played out.

My path took a big leap forward when I started working with a sponsor who said, "My job as your sponsor is for me to put you in the hand of God."

You and God

The second element in the money detox process is all about spirituality. Let's get clear right up front: if you want to change your money mindset, you need to be willing to embrace the spiritual dimension of this work. Healing starts with spirituality. I see God's hand in my life and in anyone else's. I believe your relationship with a higher power is part and parcel of any meaningful solution you will find in your life.

Now, when I speak about "God," that is just my term. You don't have to use the same word or even have the same concept I have. What matters is having the recognition of some form of higher power that is greater than your limited self, one you can turn to. However you wish to conceive of a higher power is entirely up to you. You may call it God. You may call it Consciousness. You may call it the Universe. You may call it Spirit. You may call it Higher Power. The name doesn't matter. Any of those is fine. Or whatever else you might prefer. In fact, I find that most people I meet have some understanding of spirituality, even if they explain it in terms of science.

Again, I refer you to the 12 steps of Alcoholics Anonymous. Acknowledging a higher power is built into the premise of that approach. It's an unabashedly faith-based approach to alcoholism and other addictions, and its principles apply equally when it comes to money problems.

Money shame is a spiritual crisis that requires a spiritual awakening. If you think you can get away with anything less, you're kidding yourself.

Tough Love

God sent Amrita to me at the right time in my life. She was a compassionate friend and a mentor and a strong support. She gave me tough love, at times. She wouldn't let me fall back into a victim space. What I learned from her informs how I coach others now. Like Amrita, I don't let people go far into a victim space. I shut it down fast and return them to empowerment.

When people come to me for coaching, I say, "I'm going to tell you the truth about your behavior. Sometimes you're not going to like me, but I'm always going to talk to you from a place of love. I'm not going to make you wrong. Or shame you. The truth has the power to set you free from your pain. Trust me, hang in there, and keep moving forward."

And they always do.

I often see clients who are stuck in the places I used to be stuck. One of the first steps is having the willingness to recognize you don't have the answers. It's okay that you don't. Admitting that your best thinking got you into the situation you're in frees you to be willing to learn something new. That is true humility!

Perhaps the new thing you have to do is something scary, such as asking for help or showing up in a support group or going to therapy or attending a retreat. Have the willingness to keep walking through growth when shame doesn't want to let you. Humility, willingness, and self-compassion are the spiritual trifecta that will empower you to walk a path of love and forgiveness toward ultimate healing.

Transformation Arrives

One of the laws of the universe is that for every action, there is an equal and opposite reaction. When it comes to money, this law can manifest without delay. People have this idea that it's delayed: "I can be dishonest, and it won't catch up to me." That's just not true. It does catch up. It will catch up. Often sooner than you think.

When I was out of integrity with money, I simply was not honest with myself about my behavior with money. I spent more than I was earning, until that forced me into bankruptcy. I needed a massive disruption to get my attention. My thinking was so dishonest. I believed I could keep up these shenanigans and get away with it. I could keep spending, and somebody would rescue me. Somebody would get me out of any mess I created for myself. I didn't think twice about putting something on a credit card. It was all about delay. Delay. Delay. Delay. I thought I could just keep delaying the payments. I could keep delaying what I owed.

When the market crashed in 2008 and my business shut down, I had to use credit. I started playing credit card bingo. I told myself I needed to use credit because I couldn't possibly change my lifestyle. I couldn't skip dinner with my girlfriends. I had to pick up the tab and keep pretending I was some bigshot. But those dinners became progressively more stressful. I was beyond living paycheck to paycheck, because there was no longer a paycheck coming in. I was relying strictly on credit and my dwindling savings.

I would go out to dinner with my girlfriends. The bill would arrive, and I'd start to sweat. I'd pull out my credit card and add it to the pile of cards stacked on top of the bill to divide the check among us. As the server swooped in to remove the stack, I'd appear to engage in happy chatter with my girlfriends, but inside I'd be going into a full-scale panic attack. I would pray to God that when the server came back with that neat little stack of credit cards, mine had gone through.

Let me be clear, that kind of prayer is not what I mean when I talk about the hand of God. That was me bargaining with God. That was me trying to put one over on God. That was me denying that I was in spiritual crisis.

There is a situation I like to call the *grocery line of decline.* It happens when you know you're super close to your credit limit, or you're down to just a couple of bucks in your account. You need some items from the grocery store, but those pesky balances don't stop you from running to the store. Magical thinking kicks in. Somehow you'll have enough. You count the dollars and the pennies as you agonize over what to put in and what to remove from your cart. You hope you get it right because once you're in the checkout line, you don't want to hear, "I'm sorry, but there appears to be something wrong with your card. It's been declined." There's something wrong all right: there isn't enough money in your account to pay for those essentials.

Now when clients come in, you better believe I can recognize and empathize with credit card bingo and the grocery line of decline. Because I experienced those hellholes, I can spot anyone under that kind of spell.

Before things could get better for me, they had to get worse. I had to hit rock bottom. After I lost everything in the financial crisis, I understood why Keith had taken his life. I felt as if I couldn't face the world because I had failed in every single category in which my family put credence.

I was broke.

I was in debt.

I had no job.

I had no relationship.

I did not look good.

I needed nothing less than a revolution in my life. And that's exactly what I got when I started working with Amrita. At that time, Amrita was living a few doors down from me. She is someone who is always full of love and joy, and is a badass feminist. I liked and admired all that about her, but I hadn't told her what was really going on in my life. I was too filled with shame to do that.

Until one day, it all came spilling out.

I could see Amrita growing shocked as I relayed my story. "Tam, I've seen you every day," she said. "Every single day! And you never said anything to me. You never told me anything that was going on with you. I could have helped you!"

Amrita quickly became my most significant catalyst for change. As I said, God sent her at the right time in my life. She was a truth teller, and it wasn't always easy to hear what she had to say. But I trusted her and realized that to heal, I had to be willing to examine what she said to me. Rather than close off, shut down, curl up, and die, I remained willing to hear her words and ask myself if they were valid. Was I a victim? Was I crying and whining?

I was thirty-eight at the time. I was sober from alcohol and drugs. I'd spent the last fifteen years in self-help, including therapy, retreats, and 12-step treatment centers for different issues, including drugs and alcohol, codependency, incest survivor, and love addiction. I'd had various mentors and sponsors over the years. But when I started working with Amrita, I was shocked to discover I had no clue about all the pain and shame hidden deep inside me.

Despite my long list of help-seeking actions, I had never really done the work. I had never surrendered all my addictive behaviors. My money was my identity. I had to lose my money and go through all the pain and suffering that caused before I could finally reach a place of willingness to surrender. Only when I could no longer hide behind money could I start my crawl toward health.

The key to my inner revolution was realizing that what I thought was a money crisis was really a spiritual crisis. The real problem wasn't money. It was the state of my spiritual life. As I worked with Amrita, I began to understand that if I could clean up my act with God, then everything else would fall into place.

Amrita introduced me to God through meditation and chanting, which elevated me to another level of consciousness. Through meditation, I was able to see the behavior and patterns of my mind. I was able to experience my own divine self within. I was able to learn how to control my experience of my environment rather than letting my surroundings control me. I did this with God's help. Research by Jon Kabat-Zin and others shows that meditation can have a powerful effect on mental health and well-being, including helping us cope with stress and anxiety, and increase empathy and resilience.[1] Other benefits include reducing inflammation and blood pressure

---

1. Jon Kabat-Zinn, "Mindfulness-Based Interventions in Context: Past, Present, and Future," *Clinical Psychology: Science and Practice* 10, no. 2 (2003):144–56.

as well as improving attention skills. It can even transform the brain itself. Harvard researchers found that long-term meditation can even create new gray matter in the brain, which is essential to our ability to process information.[2]

I also began doing breathwork, using breathing exercises to improve my mental, physical, and spiritual health. Breathwork releases suppressed memories and traumas in the body. It quickly brought awareness to my unconscious beliefs and patterns of behavior. Once identified, I could clear them.

As part of my yoga practice, I learned about the chakra system. The first chakra (root chakra) is the energy center located at the base of your spine. This point on the body is about survival. When your root chakra energy is in balance, you feel safe about your future and grounded about your past. This chakra permits you to feel abundant when you're grounded, but if this energy center is blocked, then a scarcity mentality can take hold.

While adding all these practices to my life, I put down pursuing women. I put down pursuing money. I put down pursuing more material things. Instead, I went after God—which meant I was pursuing my own inner self.

I'm going to repeat that because I want to make sure you

2. Britta K. Hölzel, James Carmody, Mark Vangel, Christina Congleton, Sita M. Yerramsetti, Tim Gard, and Sara W. Lazar,. "Mindfulness Practice Leads to Increases in Regional Brain Gray Matter Density," *Psychiatry Research* 191, no. 1 (2011): 36–43.

get it: *I went after God, which meant I was pursuing my own inner self.*

That was a paradigm shift for me—a love addict in constant pursuit of the feeling of being loved. The way I had been living, the minute my stash of love ran out, I'd find someone new to keep the feeling of being loved alive inside me. After about ninety days of a new relationship, it would start running out, and I'd be on to the next person.

When I described my loneliness to Amrita, she would say, "It's not a woman, and it's not money. You're longing for God. You're longing for yourself. You have to be alone for a while. You can't get into another relationship."

As I grew in spiritual practice and education, what I experienced on my journey was beyond anything I could ever have imagined. Nobody could have convinced me that I would have such miraculous experiences. And if they tried, I wouldn't have believed them. Now, I actually began to have little moments during the day when I felt relief. This was a monumental shift for someone like me who had been living in a chronic state of fear, worry, and anxiety for as long as I could remember.

I began doing a lot of writing, which helped me discover truths about myself that I hadn't been able to see or admit before. The only thing I did differently was to pray and ask God to show me the truth about myself. While I was writing, I felt a comforting presence with me. No longer did

I feel all alone in the world; now I felt I had a partner in God. A partner to help me help myself.

I learned that I could ask God to show me the right next action. Yes, action. When it comes to our finances, we have to get out, show up, and work hard. Faith without work is useless. Even after growing up Catholic and attending private school for seven years, the idea of asking God to show me the truth felt foreign to me. I had never understood that God was a co-creator with me. Nor did I understand that trusting and relying on God was the way out of my manic mind and neuroses. This concept that I could have a connection with something outside my mind was, well, mind-blowing. I was always in my head, my intellect. As I wrote and prayed, and prayed and wrote, I began to experience increasing relief. I stopped checking my bank account balance multiple times a day. That was a true miracle!

Carol and Anthony's Story

I met Carol at a networking event where I was a guest speaker on money beliefs and shame. She approached me afterwards and said, "My husband and I make $90,000 year, and we have $90,000 in credit card debt. Can you help us?"

Anthony came into my office the following Friday night armored up with two pistols, a knife, and ammo under his belt. He was six feet tall, bald with a goatee, tatted up, and husky, and had a killer resting face. He had an energy drink in one hand and a chunk of dip under his lip. He was a Red Sox fan, and I couldn't help but see my brother Keith in him right away. Carol had the energy of a high school cheerleader, with a mean-girl edge.

This pair had a real "screw you" attitude. Anthony told me later that he'd said to Carol on the way over, "If I smell one piece of bullshit, we're walking out." But I had them at hello: it was love at first sight all around.

I had ninety minutes to gain their trust and explain where I could take them, with their cooperation. My first question was how they spent their $90,000 annual income.

They shared that they spent their weekends touring all the Ross stores in Central Florida. They had no rent because Anthony worked as a property manager, and absent any housing costs, they spent their money shopping and taking cruises. When I presented my concept of the money detox, I was met with a little bit of resistance. Spirituality wasn't their cup of tea, you could say. But Carol wanted to give it a try, so they agreed to meet every Friday night for the next twelve months.

I told Carol and Anthony at our first meeting that nothing was going to get better until they got into integrity with their money. In my view, it's impossible to stay on any spiritual path if you don't live with integrity. Yet these two had an entrenched belief that it was their right to say, "Screw the man. Screw the government." They refused to pay what they owed. They were out of integrity, yet they couldn't understand why integrity wasn't flowing their way.

I know that anyone with $90,000 in consumer credit card debt is in a lot of pain about the past. Over time, I learned that Carol came from a very religious home and had gotten pregnant at sixteen. She was sent away to live at a center for girls, where she chose to give her child up for adoption. Carol never felt fully accepted by her peers after returning to school and never forgave herself for her actions. In her early twenties, she remarried and had a second child, only to divorce and raise her son as a single mom. Her guilt and shame resulted in compulsive spending and food addiction to numb the pain.

Anthony was on his third marriage and had two daughters from his first wife. He moved to Florida for a job opportunity, leaving his children, and with the impression from his ex-wife that he would see them often. However, his ex-wife changed the rules and cut off regular visits with his children. He was in a lot of pain from not being able to see his daughters grow up. When I met Anthony, he had been in Florida for eight years at a job he hated. But he stayed because he felt trapped and powerless over his financial situation.

Carol and Anthony were willing to do the work needed to turn their lives around. They did the in-depth self-inquiry, examining their money shame, beliefs, family history, forgiveness, and self-compassion. It took us every bit of ten months to clean out the past, clean up their credit reports, and turn around their money belief systems. They paid down $40,000 in consumer credit card debt in just one year!

At one point, they felt stuck. I actually believe there is no such thing as being stuck, as we are always growing, even when it feels like we're sinking. So I suggested a home visit. I knew I had to inspire them to clear out the old because they wanted desperately to move to a more desirable home. I also had a hunch about what might be preventing their movement. I suggested that they might be living in a way that was out of integrity.

They didn't agree with me. Their exact response was "Screw the spiritual."

That's when I said I was coming over to do the cleanup work with them and prove that this shit worked.

I went in with no judgment, and to this day they say they can't believe they let me see the inside of their home. They didn't trust anybody, and Anthony had the arsenal of guns to prove it. Although I had prepared myself for a bad scene, I had underestimated their living conditions. As I suspected, they were hoarders. Working together that day, I was able to show them how, on every level, they were buried in their past. The bags of items we took out of that house were stuffed with their histories: all the things they hadn't forgiven themselves for. All their items from their previous marriages were there. We filled the entire bed of Anthony's

Ford F-150 pickup truck with garbage bags of clothes and stuff to donate. Getting rid of it all expanded them in a way that allowed them to get into more integrity with their money.

I had been empowering them all that first year, telling them that the way to move along was to address and clean up the past, pay what they owed, and eliminate all the stuff that was holding them down and keeping them stuck. As I predicted, after that clean-up day, Anthony ended up changing careers and made a good move to the restaurant business, while Carol also took a new job. They moved to their dream house. Carol's relationship with both her children is now flourishing. Anthony has lost sixty pounds and doesn't resemble the man I met on that first Friday night.

Carol, Anthony, and I have very different views of the world. We were able to find common ground in our shared money shame stories. We lived in vulnerability and courage every Friday night as we cried, laughed, got angry, and felt grief around every topic imaginable. This all started with a conversation about money, and it all came together when Carol and Anthony finally embraced the spiritual dimension of their lives.

Kyle's Story

When I met Kyle, he told me he had half a million dollars of debt from what he owed on student loans, on credit cards, and to the IRS. He said, "I feel like I'm headed for a nervous breakdown and I'm only twenty-seven."

Kyle was raised by a single mother in a low-income home. Life was stressful. He was bullied at school. He was on the hefty side, shy, and smart—the perfect trifecta for bullies. To cover up his feelings of shame and pain, he turned to food and video games, and as he got older, he added fancy cars and cruises to impress his friends and family.

In his money detox process, Kyle began to unpack his money story. He could see that his spending was a symptom of not fitting in, not belonging, not feeling worthy. He had learned this coping strategy as a kid and it had served him well at the time, perhaps even saved this life. But it was having the opposite impact on his adult life. Now he had much bigger emotional, social, financial, and spiritual problems. It was time to practice a new way of living.

As part of his money detox, Kyle needed some new tools to help with his compulsive behaviors. I believe everyone has some idea what to do to get relief in the moment, so I asked Kyle, "What do you really want to do that serves you when your fear and panic come up?"

"I want to just lie back and picture the beach, with the

waves crashing all around me, the warm sun on my face, my feet in the sand."

Maybe he thought that he was just suggesting an escape fantasy. But that's not at all how I saw it. I said, "Wonderful! Every time you want to shop on Amazon or buy a new game, pause instead. Take a deep breath and go to your happy place. Picture yourself on the beach. Give it a try. I'll bet you find it works."

Kyle took this practice to heart, and it helped him tremendously. For the first time in his life, he could feel peace. It started with five minutes, then grew to fifteen minutes, then thirty minutes. Without labeling it as something "spiritual," he had introduced meditation into his life. Soon it was flowing into his whole day. He got a better-paying job, which allowed him to cut his spending proportionately in half. He began paying down his debt and saving. It all started with taking five minutes to close his eyes, lie on the beach, and just breathe.

Finding Your God

Here is a question for you: what are your gods?

I mean your real gods—what you worship in your life.

Do your gods include money, work, academic pursuits, success, sex, looking good, social media obsessions, relationships, shopping, care taking, alcohol, drugs, food, video games, exercise, or religion?

Can you identify with anything in this list? Do any of these areas dominate your thinking, your emotions, or your actions? Are you the master of your money or are your money and possessions mastering you?

When you recognize that money isn't the root problem, and you acknowledge that what is really happening to you is a spiritual crisis, then you have to start answering questions such as these. You have to find what God, or a higher power, is for you.

I can't tell you what that power is for you. That's different for each person. As it should be. What I can do is describe what I found when I went looking for God.

I had to understand the role shame was having on my self-worth. I did not believe I was worthy enough to have an all-loving, powerful God. It took losing all my money to learn how to quiet my mind so I could trust and rely on my intuition. As I did, I found that God came through me and through each of us. I'm a part of God. You're a part of God. We're not separate. We are one. We're all connected. I can see the face of God in everyone I meet. I'd been a doubter all my life because of shame, so I had to have concrete proof multiple times to become a believer in a loving God who really has my back. Today, I know a real sense of belonging, which feels like nothing short of a miracle.

"What does God have to do with anything?" you ask.

"Everything," I reply. I say that because it is my

experience. I believe God's plan for us is to have all the money we can spend—the kingdom, not the scraps.

To enter that kingdom—which is none other than our own being—we have to do the work of self-inquiry and we have to trust. It all starts with realizing that a spiritual crisis needs a spiritual solution. We can't fix money problems with money.

SELF-DIRECTION #2: Spirituality Inventory

Pull out your money journal and write about these questions. Keep in mind that there aren't any right or wrong answers.

- What role did spirituality have in my family growing up?

- What name do I use for a higher power?

- How important is spirituality in my life now?

- How can I make it more important or a priority?

- Who is a spiritual mentor for me? Who can I ask?

- What is the relationship between spirituality and money in my life?

- How can I strengthen it?

3

Uncover Your Shame

Having been poor is no shame. Being ashamed of it is.

— Benjamin Franklin

Shame can be a crushing emotion. It makes us feel weak and small and unworthy and helpless. When it relates to money, shame can be the leading sign of a disorder that paralyzes all aspects of your life. Brad Klontz and his colleagues have done a lot of groundbreaking work around money disorders, which they define as "maladaptive patterns of financial beliefs and behaviors that lead to clinically significant distress, impairment in social or occupational functioning, undue financial strain, or an inability to enjoy one's financial resources."[1] They created

---

1. Brad T. Klontz, A. Bivens, P. Klontz, J. Wada, and R. Kahler, "The Treatment of

an assessment tool to help professionals identify money disordered behaviors, including pathological gambling, overspending and compulsive buying, underspending and compulsive hoarding, workaholism, financial dependence, financial enabling, financial denial/rejection, and financial enmeshment.

Despite that research, however, financial advice books typically discuss the problem and then proceed to direct you to respond at what I would describe as a relatively superficial level. They offer the type of advice I gave Keith and Karen at our Starbucks meeting: spend less, save more, diversify your portfolio, buy term insurance, and invest the rest. Is that sound advice? On the surface, sure. But for many of us, mere knowledge is not enough, and *more* knowledge is not always helpful. In fact, it can be overwhelming. In the years since Keith's death, in working with clients, I've created a more humanistic approach to addressing money issues, one that goes to the core of the problem—that is, the spiritual crisis that masquerades as a purely financial problem in our lives.

Disordered Money Behaviors: Results of an Open Clinical Trial," *Psychological Services* 5, no. 3 (2008):295-308.

How Much of our Mind is Conscious?

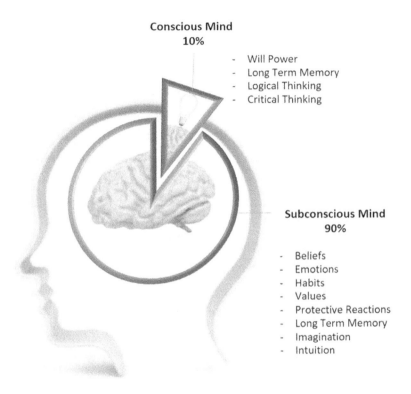

Conscious Mind
10%

- Will Power
- Long Term Memory
- Logical Thinking
- Critical Thinking

Subconscious Mind
90%

- Beliefs
- Emotions
- Habits
- Values
- Protective Reactions
- Long Term Memory
- Imagination
- Intuition

At least 90 percent of our beliefs, emotions, and habits are subconscious. That means you are not aware of most of the feelings and the ideas and beliefs you have about money. On a daily basis, you are acting out of and reacting to your feelings about money, but without ever being aware of the origin of those feelings. Fortunately, the content of the subconscious mind is not under lock and key. It is possible through self-inquiry to uncover your hidden feelings and underlying beliefs and change them. Using my unique experience; training; and blend of financial, psychological, and spiritual practices, I will teach you how to let go of fear and frenzy and how to make peace with your money and achieve freedom. This simple process can provide you and your family with lasting results for generations to come.

In my experience, the first thing that jumps out when people with money problems start to tell their money story is usually shame. In fact, shame is what keeps us from telling our stories in the first place. As we begin to own our story, it is only natural that shame would show up. Therefore, the third element in the money detox process focuses on uncovering shame in a manner that can defuse and resolve it. As we will discuss, this includes distinguishing between toxic shame and healthy shame.

First, however, let me share how toxic shame entered my life and how it spread.

Looking at My Legacy of Shame

Established in 1729, Westford, Massachusetts, could have been a backdrop in a Norman Rockwell painting. But the view depended on where you stood. Westford was firmly divided into two distinct tiers: the bottom of the hill, which was populated by blue-collar mill workers, and the markedly white-collar top of the hill. In addition to the geographical divide, Westfordians were either Protestant or Catholic, and quite religiously segregated, at that.

My mother's parents, Joan and Paul, were second-generation Catholic immigrants from Poland and England who settled down in Westford and worked hard for the American dream. Although they were low income, they were not poor. Joan hailed from a big Irish-Polish family and had eleven siblings. Despite the family's work ethic, she grew up with a tremendous amount of physical, emotional, and spiritual abuse. She was riddled with shame; in fact, it was somewhat standard practice in her generation to be parented and controlled by shame.

My grandmother Joan learned that despite what she was feeling inside, it was of the utmost importance to look good on the outside, to present an acceptable appearance to others, to always consider what others might think. My grandfather Paul was an Irish bar brawler. Their money story was that you had to work hard, as your work was your value. Period. The conversation at any family gathering would inevitably be about work, work, and work.

My father's German/Irish/English family was entirely different. My grandmother Helen was not a traditional woman for the times. She wore pantsuits in the 1920s, for example. She was a powerful woman but was manipulative and abusive to my father when he was a child. My father, like my mother, grew up with a lot of shame and codependency. The money messages were more of the same: You work. You look good. Your work is your value. Your money is your worth.

In 1965, my nineteen-year-old father got my eighteen-year-old mother pregnant while she was still in high school. This was the worst kind of shame in my mother's Catholic family: a pregnancy out of wedlock. My grandmother no longer looked good with a knocked-up high schooler. The story goes that when she discovered the pregnancy, she almost beat my mother to death with a statue of the Virgin Mary (you can't make this up), requiring my uncle to intervene to save his sister's life.

My father's mother took the situation in hand and decided to make the pregnancy right. She marched the two teenagers off to the county courthouse, where they were immediately married. Helen paid for the young couple to move to the top of the hill, into the servants' quarters of a large mansion that had been home to one of the founding fathers of the town. My father was a bit of an elitist and considered himself better than the lot at the bottom of the hill. He revelled in the idea of living in a mansion (albeit in the servants' quarters), from where he could look down upon everyone below. Helen agreed to pay their rent.

My father was already a budding alcoholic at the time of their wedding. Within a few years, the young couple had three children in quick Catholic succession, with me being the last. By the time I entered the picture, as if alcoholism weren't bad enough, my father had become addicted to heroin. He was a complete mess, and in no condition to support a growing family. He physically abused my mother and cheated on her. My father was a selfish addict who often left the family for days at a time with no money and very little food. My mother soon found herself in a chronic state of "not enough." Her shame was the noose around her young neck, keeping her from asking for family help. She chose instead to live paycheck to paycheck. She did her best to cover up her growing fear and angst by looking good to the outside world. My two brothers, James and Keith, and I were born into this loop of shame and dysfunction at the top of the hill.

After five years of marriage, my mother'd had enough. She locked my father out of the servants' quarters and announced that they were through. He promptly left town, abandoning my mother to raise three kids, with no financial assistance, in a wealthy Catholic suburb. That was not supposed to be part of the plan, and my mother was devastated by the turn of events. She couldn't believe he didn't want to be a parent, and she internalized the idea that he didn't love her and their children enough to shape up. The only love she'd ever known was my father's. When he deserted her, not only did she miss her partner, but she was left alone to take on responsibility for the family's emotional, physical, spiritual, and financial tabs. That was a hefty bill for a young, uneducated, single mother of three to pay.

The shame in our family was in the blood, handed down from mother to father to son to daughter. The men were brutal. They tended to be painfully sarcastic and teasing, but it was of course never funny when you happened to be the object of that vicious humor. The women were consummate artists, painting pretty exterior landscapes of their lives solely for the benefit of others. But those pictures looked nothing like the reality lurking behind the slam of every one of their front doors. The women were the archetypes who carried the load of shame, passing it down from generation to generation, like a hot potato.

The Birth of Toxic Shame

My mother married Peter for money and security, not for love. We all knew that.

When Peter entered the picture, he rolled out the red carpet and struck up the band. He spoiled my mother. He bought her a car. He lavished her with fancy gifts, such as a fur coat and beautiful clothes. He bought her both a top-of-the-line record player and 8-track player (high-tech at the time). He gave her everything she'd ever wanted. My brothers and I weren't left behind. He bought us expensive clothes and brand-new toys that we wouldn't otherwise have been able to afford. In hindsight, it was his way of grooming us for the abuse to come.

He appeared to adore my mother, and who could blame

him? She was quite a stunner. The fact that he was willing to date a divorced single mom with three kids made him a real hero in the eyes of just about everyone, especially my birth father, who said at the time, "I have a lot of respect for a guy willing to take on three kids and a wife." What my father meant, but didn't say, was that he had a lot of respect for a guy who was willing to take on the financial responsibility of his three kids and his ex-wife, allowing my father to swim free of the financial hook. Initially, we all felt Peter was the answer to our prayers, a real dream come true: *now we would have money, and everything would be okay.*

I didn't know anything about class or social standing when I was young—at least not in my early youth—and I didn't need to. Despite our lodging in the servants' quarters, I was embraced by all the kids in the neighborhood. By the time I entered fifth grade, I was in with the cool kids and included in all the birthday parties and other celebrations. We called ourselves The Gang. It was the first year of middle school, and at nine years old, I felt like I was starting the year off strong. With Peter's financial help, our home life had improved, as well. No longer did my mother appear to be feeling quite so financially stressed. Even though we didn't own our home, we at least had some of the trappings that were important at the time.

One cool, crisp October afternoon, The Gang walked home from school together, laughing and kicking at the piles of leaves that signaled the oncoming change of seasons. One of the girls, Alicia, invited us to her house for an impromptu pumpkin-carving party. Secretly, I was excited to be included in this spontaneous invitation because she lived in one of the grand historic homes in the area, and I'd never been inside before. I'd often wondered what it must be like to live in such a mansion.

As we eagerly piled in through the massive kitchen's side door, reserved for the service people, cooks, and cleaners, Alicia's mother came around the corner, pointed directly at me, and said, "You! Go stand in the driveway."

There was an uncomfortable silence, and I stood there for a heartbeat, unsure if she was speaking to me. She couldn't possibly be speaking to me. I didn't know her. I'd never met her before. I hadn't done anything to her. But when she locked eyes with me, refusing to drop her pointed finger, I stumbled backward amidst the other girls.

What had just happened? Had I done something wrong?

Outside, I shivered in the cold, gathering gloom of that fall afternoon, which just moments before had been rife with possibility. As the leaves fluttered lazily down from the tall trees, sprinkling the driveway with golds and reds and browns, two of the girls walked outside to stand on either side of me. They urged me not to pay any attention to our friend's mother, but that did not take away the sting of her words. I only felt worse, because I was so utterly embarrassed. I'd been singled out from my peers and shamed before them for reasons I didn't yet understand. I was not even given a name. I was simply called *You!* The pain was as sharp as if that rich lady had stuck a dagger into my soul. Which, in fact, she had.

That incident only lasted a couple of moments, but it burned into my subconscious mind and created a level of pain I wasn't even aware existed. I was in that pain until my forties, although it was on a completely subconscious level.

My money shame was birthed that moment. I hadn't been born with whatever nebulous right would have allowed me entrance into that mansion. I didn't have the right last name. The proper clothing. The correct history. The famous family. To my young mind, this made me wrong—as in, something was wrong with me. Being ordered from the service wing of that home meant I was beneath even the lowly workers that lady paid to clean her dishes and launder her underwear.

The social economics of Westford said that because my mom's family lived at the bottom of the hill in the blue-collar Catholic section of town, those were my roots. That was who I was. The rich lady felt I needed to be firmly reminded of who I was and where I came from. She wanted to make sure I knew my place.

That afternoon in fifth grade was my first experience with toxic shame, with the feeling that something was fundamentally wrong with me. That was my first understanding that I wasn't like some other people. I was different, and different was inferior.

I didn't tell my mother what had happened. It was unlikely she could have done anything to assuage my shame. Instead, I internalized that experience. It sank into my subconscious, where it substantiated a deep-seated belief that my worth was equal to money. Which meant I wasn't worth much. I swallowed that entire experience, allowing it to take root, bloom, blossom, and spread—even as I wasn't aware at the time that that was what was happening.

The Toxic Shame Spreads

The toxic shame lurking in my subconscious manifested in different ways and in different areas of my life over the next few years. It was pervasive.

In the summer of 1978, when I was ten years old, the movie *Grease*, starring Olivia Newton-John and John Travolta, made its debut. I loved that movie! I loved all the singing and the storyline, as it fed right into my hopeless romantic fantasy mindset. I must have seen the movie a dozen times. I was obsessed. The last scene at the carnival was my favorite part because Sandy got a makeover from Frenchy and was transformed from a wholesome good girl into a cigarette-smoking leather-pants-wearing bad girl to attract her beloved, Danny. It wasn't until I heard my girlfriends giggling over Danny that I realized I was different in yet another way—because I was awestruck over Olivia Newton-John (in those tight black leather pants) and not John Travolta. Did that mean I liked girls more than boys? This discovery became a place of deep shame for me for many years to come. Thirty-five years, to be exact.

What does this have to do with money?

Everything. In my Catholic home, being gay was a source of shame. I used money to cover it up. I believed I was bad. As I grew older, I used anything to fill the hole: shoes, cars, chocolate, travel and women.

Money was worshipped in my home. Money was our god. It was the solution to every problem. The only way out of shame was to buy your way out. My mother didn't have the grit to find a better way out because she grew up in shame. Her mother grew up in shame and passed it down to my mother, just like her brown eyes and shoe size. I've often wondered during my journey what chance my mother even had to break the cycle. Her peers didn't question the way things were in the way that my generation now does.

One of the first things Peter did when he took up with my mother was to eliminate my father from the picture. "I will take care of your ex and your kids," he privately told him. "But I don't ever want to see your face. You get the hell out of town and don't bother us ever again." My father, gleefully relieved of the potential financial burden of his family, skedaddled out of our lives, never to return.

Next, Peter asked my mother to leave our safe suburb in Westford and move out of the area. He and his brother had gotten into a fight and broken up their building business, so he had grand plans to start anew somewhere else. He moved to Virginia immediately, as my mother pressed him to get established before we would follow. After three years, she decided to uproot the three of us and join Peter in Maryland, where he was by then. I was twelve; Keith was fourteen; and our older brother, James, was fifteen. The move itself was very traumatic as we didn't know anything but the small town of Westford. The working-class black neighborhood in Maryland where we landed was entirely new to us. It sounds ridiculous, but the world was a different place back then. We didn't have any black friends at home, as things were still racially divided in the early 1970s.

My mother didn't listen to the advice of anybody in her family. My aunt, uncle, and grandmother each told her they didn't think Peter was right for her. They begged her not to uproot her kids. But in her mind, what choice did she have? She needed the financial help of a partner, of a man, of a co-parent. Raising three kids on her own was proving to be more than she could handle. As we became teenagers, we were only growing more expensive to support. When my mother decided to join Peter despite her family's misgivings, her mother said, "You make your bed, you lie in it." And so my mother's fate was sealed, along with ours. No matter what happened, we would not be welcomed back to Westford.

It was probably not a surprise to anyone but us that Peter had lied to my mother. We didn't move into that big, beautiful house he had promised was waiting for us in Maryland. The savings and loan industry had recently collapsed, and since Peter was in the building industry, every loan on his houses had been called. He was rendered bankrupt overnight, leaving him with a hefty debt owed to the IRS. That was a lot of money back then, a seemingly insurmountable amount of debt.

Three months after we joined Peter in Maryland, my mother discovered she was pregnant. It appeared that Peter wasn't sterile, as he had claimed. With the pregnancy in place, he trapped her, and by default, my brothers and I were caught, as well. What an absolute mess all our lives then became. Thomas was born prematurely and remained in the hospital for the first three months of his life. My mother was in a dire situation, with a new baby with medical needs, and no money, no safety, and no security—and she'd inherited Peter's financial train wreck. The mantra running through her head was *You make your bed, you lie in it.*

Peter started molesting me when I turned thirteen. There was no safe space in our new home. Peter was everywhere, his desire overt, creepy, stalkerish, and inescapable. As I watched my mother's life fall to pieces, I knew I couldn't tell her what was happening. How could I add one more thing to her burden? What kind of daughter would I be to do that to my already embattled mother?

I wondered later why I didn't tell anyone what was happening to me. It was, I realized, because I had internalized the sexual abuse to be my fault. Around that same time, I became a love addict. Even though the attention I garnered was false, negative, and harmful, it was better than nothing. When I did get into therapy years later and finally said that out loud, I was with a group of women who also had been sexually abused. We talked about how we had so much shame. We beat ourselves up mercilessly. *Maybe I should have said something when it was happening? I should have spoken up! It was my responsibility to do something, and I didn't.*

Many people don't get help because they share that line of reasoning, and it plays into shame like a fiddle. Secrecy and silence are what shame needs to grow. Having sexual abuse as part of the story trains us to be silent.

As the pressure and responsibility for his new family mounted, Peter became progressively more abusive. The generosity gig at the outset of his relationship with my mother appeared to be nothing more than a ruse. We discovered that he was indeed a nasty guy, super controlling, and very mean to my teenage brothers. Both my older brothers got into alcohol and drugs to cope. This was hardest on Keith, and he declined rapidly. Feeling scared about the shifting changes, he cried all the time. Even though money was tight, my mother gave all of us the opportunity to attend private school. She was willing to make that sacrifice. I accept her offer, but my brothers refused. In hindsight, it was her one act of grit that may have saved me.

Peter didn't allow my mother to work. She had no money of her own, and he refused to give her any. My brothers and I had babysitting jobs and other odd jobs, so we secretly gave her money. In high school, James became a drug dealer and helped pay the rent with his illegal gains when money was tight. I don't know how Peter justified in his mind that his stepchildren were financially supporting the family, but Peter and my mother allowed it to happen. She forged an alliance with her children: us against Peter. My brothers and I paid the bills, while Peter screamed at us that we were my mother's kids and we were pieces of shit. Despite this outrageous financial dynamic, when I was a teenager, money was always tight in our home. My stepfather was a tyrant when it came to money. We represented money to him. We cost him money, and shame was one of the main ways he made us pay.

Toxic Shame and Shame Resilience

In her groundbreaking book *I Thought It Was Just Me (But It Isn't)*, Brené Brown says shame is "the intensely painful feeling or experience of believing we are flawed and therefore unworthy of acceptance and belonging."[2] This is a feeling that is very familiar to me, even if I spent years denying it. Perhaps to you, as well.

But is shame necessarily bad? Some argue that no form of shame can be considered good in any way. However, Silvan Tomkins, who first coined the term *toxic shame syndrome* in the 1960s, describes shame as one among the full range of human emotions.[3] According to this view, we all experience shame at some time or other when something that we do, and that we thought should go well, doesn't. Or we make a mistake that embarrasses us. This kind of healthy shame is a temporary feeling, and doesn't undermine your sense of self-worth.

Someone who has healthy shame might say:

- "Oops, I should never have done that. I'm so sorry! Totally my bad."

- "You're right: that was really inconsiderate of me. I feel like an idiot. I promise, I won't do it again."

- "I should never have bought that expensive necklace. You'll be happy to hear I returned it."

Common qualities of healthy shame, as you can see here,

2. Brené Brown, *I Thought It Was Just Me (But It Isn't): Telling the Truth About Perfectionism, Inadequacy, and Power* (New York: Penguin, 2008).
3. See the Tomkins Institute website, http://www.tomkins.org/what-tomkins-said/introduction/positive-affects-when-interrupted-yield-to-the-affect-of-shame/

include the ability to admit one's mistakes, self-acceptance, humility, the willingness to apologize, and knowing how to let go and move on. In other words, healthy shame is really more like remorse than what we typically think of as shame.

In contrast, toxic shame is shame that has gone underground. People with toxic shame are unlikely to talk about it in any of the above ways; in fact, they are unlikely to talk about it at all. Instead, toxic shame burrows into their psyche and stays there, and ruins their lives. To hear its voice, you would have to listen to the person's thoughts. They might go something like this:

- "I didn't just make that mistake. I couldn't have. It didn't happen."

- "I ate the entire carton in one sitting. I'm just a disgusting pig. Everyone hates me."

- "If I go into bankruptcy, I can never show my face in that town again. My life will be over."

It's obvious why such thoughts are toxic. There is no redeeming value to them. Toxic shame festers because the person who has it is utterly convinced there is no solution, no way out. For this reason, there is often a direct relationship between toxic shame and suicidal thoughts and even suicide.

Toxic money shame is nothing more than toxic shame that focuses on financial matters. This kind of shame doesn't discriminate; it doesn't care whether you're earning $10,000 a year or $10 million. You are unworthy. You are wrong. You are bad. Toxic shame will accuse you and convict without a trial. You are guilty, and your sentence is life without parole.

Money shame is the murderer of the soul. Why? Because you surrender all your power to money and then you create a cover-up to survive the unbearable pain that results. You'll do anything to deny your shame and to prevent anyone else from seeing it and whatever caused it.

Money shame cover-up behaviors include the following:

- Driving a Mercedes when you can only afford a Honda
- Playing the bigshot by always picking up the check or financially rescuing family and friends under pressure of not measuring up
- Living paycheck to paycheck
- Looking good at all costs
- Being obsessed with money, how much things cost, and how much everyone earns
- Unable to enjoy wealth
- Unable to hold onto money, continuously letting it slip through your fingers
- Getting buried in debt, yet still spending

- Going into bankruptcy, foreclosure

- Living in financial secrecy, fearing what others think of you

- Believing that knowledge is God, becoming a know-it-all

Where there's money shame, a new budget won't solve it. The only solution is one that includes uncovering your shame and dissolving it so it can't steal your sense of self-worth and net worth. Brené Brown speaks about *shame resilience* as the determining factor for who gets back up and who doesn't after being knocked down by toxic shame.[4] According to Dr. Brown, shame resilience includes recognizing shame and understanding its triggers, reaching out and telling our story, and speaking up. Shame can only thrive if we are silent and allow it to hide away in secrecy. By opening up and sharing our stories with others, we can grow our resilience by communicating and shining a light into the darkness inside.

When Dr. Brown was researching shame, she also researched people who *didn't* have shame, people who lived wholeheartedly. She looked at how they lived and what their shame looked like, and she created benchmarks for shame resilience. Her guide for developing shame resilience encourages us to embrace failure, creativity, play, laughter,

---

4. Brené Brown, *I Thought It Was Just Me.*

and self-compassion, and to do so through the practice of vulnerability.

You may come from a family system so distorted that it's completely dysfunctional. You wonder, how do I break free from shame? How do I break free from all of this shit they taught us, and come away not still feeling like I'm utterly alone in the world? How do I go against my mother? How do I do that when I was programmed to stay small, when I was programmed to always look good and be quiet?

The Money Shame Cover-Up

I often wonder why some people make the changes necessary to escape shame, and others choose not to or feel unable to do so. In fact, many people think they are escaping their shame. They think they have outwitted shame, and they are often proud because they think they did it all on their own, without ever stooping to ask anyone for help. But usually it turns out that they are the ones who have been outwitted by their own toxic shame. Because they have simply pushed the shame deeper into the subconscious and substituted other behaviors that are merely new sources of pain.

I see a pattern among those seeking to heal themselves:

- Shame develops during childhood
- Shame turns toxic

- Toxic shame needs a cover-up
- Codependent behavior provides that cover-up
- Addiction provides continued cover-up
- A false, addicted personality develops
- Addiction leads back to spending money, avoiding money, controlling money
- Money becomes the god

For the purposes of understanding and overcoming money shame, we can consider the associated problems of codependency and addiction as complications or offshoots of shame. Toxic shame needs a cover-up. It needs many avenues for cover-up. Enter codependency and addiction. Obviously not everyone who has money shame also develops codependency and/or addictions. The reverse is also true. But in my experience, the pattern is so common that I include it here, and it features prominently in my work with most clients.

As a money coach, I have discovered that codependency is at the core of most financial disfunction. Codependency has five primary symptoms: avoidance, control, low self-esteem, compliance, and denial. We experience them in opposite extremes: Having low or nonexistent self-esteem or arrogance and grandiosity. Being too vulnerable or being invulnerable. Being bad or rebellious or being good and perfect. Being too dependent or being anti-dependent or needless and wantless. Being chaotic or being controlling.

Many of us can easily see these behaviors in others but have difficulty seeing them in ourselves. Let's look at the five symptoms again and relate them to behaviors with money.

- Avoidance: not balancing the bank account or paying bills on time

- Control: using money to buy love and happiness

- Low self-esteem: spending money to feel better or look better

- Compliance: spending money on others' needs and wants while neglecting your own

- Denial: avoiding conversations about money or pretending everything is okay, while watching your car be repossessed

You can also play small by not owning your power with your money or by being controlled by a spouse or parent. You can play god with your money by recusing others financially or believing they are incapable of taking care of themselves. You can play the big shot with your money by picking up the check and needing to appear right in the eyes of others; you may even lie to look good. You can play the nice guy/gal by financially enabling your family or friends to avoid change. Lastly, you can play the victim by minimizing, rationalizing, and justifying how you truly feel, and using money to compensate.

The treatments for alcoholism/drug abuse and codependency are entirely different. One behavior is attached to toxic shame and judgment by society. The other receives praise and reward for people-pleasing. The journey out of both is a tricky bitch. It takes courage, compassion, self-love, accountability, time, patience, and practice to unravel. I can't believe I made it out alive. The tricky part about recovering from codependency is that people-pleasing is generally very acceptable behavior. In fact, I believe wholeheartedly that companies hired me when I was in my early twenties because, as a codependent, I was a hard worker and willing to put my company's needs before my own. In fact, I used to joke that the ideal assistant is an unrecovered codependent.

The Circle of Money Pain

As you go more deeply into your money story, you are likely to discover a loop. I call this the *circle of money pain*. As the illustration shows, the starting point in the circle is your inherited money beliefs. However, the telling of your money story is most likely to be driven by your emotions, rather than by an analysis of your family's beliefs. In my experience, the stories that surface first tend to be the ones that carry the greatest gut punch, and those are usually shame or shame-related incidents. Thus, the point in the circle where your awareness first falls is likely to be on shame.

The circle won't look identical for every individual, but I

present it here in the form in which I currently envision it, based on my own experience and my observations of people I've worked with. It is an evolving model that I expect to revise as my thoughts progress and change, so please view it with that in mind.

As you can see, your inherited money beliefs are at the top—the starting point—of the circle. Yet for the purposes of the money detox process, we are entering the circle at three o'clock. Each loop around the circle creates more fear, more pain, and a growing sense of powerlessness over your circumstances. You start identifying with that circle of pain. You become that circle of pain, and you can't help it because it's all you know. All you have to do to get out of this loop is to let that feeling of fear pass right through you. Sounds simple, right? But you are stuck, and you don't know how to let that fear go.

Traditionally, we have treated the symptoms of the circle of money pain like a game of whack-a-mole. We knock out one behavior and then jump straight to another. A holistic solution is necessary to treat the foundation from which all the behaviors develop. You have to let yourself feel the pain, as that is a part of the human experience. It's there to help you grow, as wisdom comes through pain. You must feel it, learn what it is there to teach you, and then let it go. If you avoid the pain—if you ignore, numb, and harbor anger and distrust and remorse toward it—you're going to wake up when you're fifty or sixty or seventy or eighty, and you're going to have to feel it. Holding onto that stress can and will cause real problems down the line—mentally, physically, and financially. Trust me, I see it every day in my office.

If you don't do something differently, you will just go around and around, endlessly circling back to the beginning. Remember, you can simply pause, ask your higher power to bring your attention to the truth about yourself, and write about it. You have the power to break the circle of pain at any moment. The key is to explore your pain by going inward.

In the chapters that follow, we will look at other parts of the circle, including your inherited money beliefs, and the way out of the circle through the power of forgiveness.

Jean's Story

I met Jean at a local bookstore and would often run into her on a weekly basis. In typical Southern fashion, we chatted about everything pleasant under the sun (except money). We had been friendly for more than a year when I received a call from her at my office. "I need help, Tammy," she confessed. "Can I come see you?"

During our first meeting, she stated that she was broke, which surprised me beyond measure. She explained she was in a whopper of a debt cycle and didn't know how to find her way out. She said that when she received her

Social Security check at the beginning of each month, she raced to the ATM and pulled out all the cash. Then she wrote checks to pay bills, resulting in hundreds of dollars of overdraft fees charged to her every month. She was always in the red—to the tune of about $2,000—and owed money to practically everyone she knew.

Jean and I had two things in common: we were Irish and we were hardheaded. So I was confident I could help! After a few questions, I developed a hunch that Jean might have access to a pension. I wasn't sure, but I went ahead and asked anyway. It turned out I was right. And I was shocked by her reply.

"I was in a professional position as a minister for twenty years, and I think I have a pension. But I screwed that up and would go to jail if I tried to claim it," she admitted sheepishly. "See, I wasn't faithful, and through the divorce decree, my ex-husband is entitled to half my pension. I haven't followed through with claiming the money, nor have I paid what I've owed him for over ten years, because I'm too pissed off at him."

My jaw dropped when I asked how much she thought her pension might be worth. "Probably about $350,000," she said, hanging her head.

As we talked more, I learned that Jean grew up in a religious home and her inherited money belief was that money was the root of all evil. After she had an affair with the man she eventually left the church for and almost married, she was overwhelmed by guilt and shame, and felt unworthy of the pension money.

Because Jean could not forgive herself or her ex-husband for what had happened thirty years ago, she allowed resentment, guilt, and shame stand in the way of her financial security. Additionally, she was still practicing the vow of poverty she had taken forty years before, resulting in a state of mind that created her poverty.

Not only that, but her emotional state was so negative due to the needless situation she'd created that she had become a compulsive overeater. Anyone could see she was heading for a heart attack.

Over the next three months, I helped Jean understand and own her money story and uncover her shame.

"Can you describe what it feels like in your body when you think about calling the pension office?" I asked.

"I feel warm and sweaty, and my heart beats fast," Jean said. "Like I just ran a race, but without any of the runner's high. I feel embarrassed and want to run and hide."

I asked her to say more about feeling embarrassed.

"I just feel so ashamed that I haven't taken care of my money responsibilities," she said. "I keep spending and spending. I don't know how I got in this mess, and it makes me feel hopeless."

"There is nothing wrong with you," I said. "I believe something happened to you in your early childhood that continues to repeat in your adulthood. We repeat what we don't repair. So let's look closer at your childhood money story. Do you remember a time when you felt shame around a circumstance with money?"

Jean described a time when she was seven years old. "I stole fifty cents from my father's wallet and ran to the store to buy candy. When I returned home, my father confronted me. He told me I was a greedy, bad, a disgrace to the family. What's worse, he said it all in front of his friends. I was mortified. He never let me forgot that experience."

As Jean went through the money detox process, she worked to let go of her shame and unworthiness. She began to shift her poverty consciousness. We also secured the $350,000 pension for her. All that required was a few phone calls, a few forms, and a few faxes. That's it. Jean found it almost impossible to believe that in choosing not to forgive herself or her ex-husband, she had created an emotional, financial, and health crisis of enormous proportions.

Jean received $55,000 in cash to pay off all her debts. She also began collecting a paycheck for life from her pension, after giving her ex-husband the half due from the divorce decree.

But that's not all. Once she had freed herself from the guilt, shame, and blame that had long hung around her neck and heart, she took a job she loved, which provided her with enough extra money to move into a lovely retirement community.

The years of neglecting her body did catch up with her,

and she suffered a massive heart attack a year after our work together. Happily, she survived and was bright enough to take her brush with death seriously. She has since repaired her relationship with her ex-husband, and in a strange and beautiful twist of fate, is now sharing a home with him, following the passing of his second wife.

Nelson and Michael's Story

Nelson and Michael had been together for five years, yet despite lots of happiness, they did not share the same beliefs about money. I initially received a phone call from Nelson, who said, "We'd like to come in and see you because my boyfriend is terrible with money, and I'm not quite sure what to do about it."

During our session, Nelson and Michael said they were questioning whether to open a joint account. I agreed it was smart of them to get a handle on what was happening in their relationship before merging their money.

It didn't take me long to explain what was immediately apparent to me: Michael was great with money; it was Nelson who was the compulsive spender. Michael lived in a lot of scarcity and fear that there wasn't going to be enough despite the fact that he earned six figures a year, lived in a modest home, did not have a car payment, and lived well beneath his means. Nelson also had a lot of fear and scarcity, but rather than live beneath his means, he covered up his fear with self-righteousness, arrogance, and displays of high intelligence. I recognized that trio as evidence of a classic case of money shame. Nelson was overly generous and often played the bigshot. He was "pennywise and pound foolish," a deadly combination.

I shared with Nelson my belief that he would benefit from individual coaching and I agreed to see Nelson and Michael as a couple in between Nelson's sessions. I knew Nelson and I had some work to do, but I didn't realize just how much. At the beginning of our work together, I could see that Nelson was suicidal. Unfortunately, I know that look all too well and see it all too often in my practice. One day I asked him at the start of our session, "Do you have a plan?"

When he replied, "Maybe," I shared a short story about my brother. I wanted to keep it light, so I included a touch of Keith's humor. Nelson broke into a big laugh that soon turned into a big, needed cry.

Nelson and I worked together for the next year, and during that time, we uncovered layer after layer of shame from his very abusive and dysfunctional family. Nelson took the courageous step to go into intensive therapy for trauma and learned to deepen his self-care. He was committed to his work and addressed his resentments, anger, separation from his family, and ultimately his need to forgive. He paid off over $30,000 in credit card debt. Then he sold his business for a profit and started his dream job. He also found God along the way and tithed regularly. Before our work together, he had been agnostic, but his journey through the money detox gave him a renewed faith in and hope for life.

Nelson and Michael are doing fantastically today and have successfully opened that joint account. They are both living their dream jobs and on purpose.

Your Money Shame

Your money shame inheritance is unlikely to step out on the sidewalk and simply declare its existence. It thrives in hiding, and that's where it's going to remain, unless you do the work to call it out. So you've got to commit to some serious self-inquiry in order to recognize and deal with your money shame. This is a crucial part of the money detox process. So let's get started!

Whenever I'm trying to uncover shame, I will sit and journal. But before I start writing, I say a short prayer. I say, "God, my past is blocking me from the sunlight of the Spirit. Please show me the truth about myself. Please write through me. Let me be your secretary." In this way, I turn it over to God. I ask for help. It is my experience that I get to the root of the shame more immediately if I ask God for help uncovering it. Then I can take the right next action to deal with whatever is happening that has led to shame. At that point, too, I ask God for help. I ask that my attention be directed toward what God would have me do.

The answers I generally get are along the lines of "Have trust" or "Let go" or "You can't control the outcome" or "This too shall pass" or "This is just a feeling; it's not the truth."

Please take from my personal example whatever resonates with you, and leave the rest. The only important thing is that you realize that your shame is a spiritual crisis that needs a spiritual solution.

In the exercise at the end of this chapter, you're going to return to the money journal you've been keeping. You may be able to use the stories you have already remembered, or you may need to recall some additional stories. The point here is to go deeper into your story. *Feel* your story.

To recap, shame is an emotion. It is the painful feeling that you are inexcusably and unforgivably wrong or worthless or in some way irreparably less than okay. In money shame, that feeling of wrongness or unworthiness is associated with money. In both cases, shame occurs in relationship to other people. Whether they really think you are wrong or worthless is not important; what matters is that you feel that way.

Jean cheated on her husband, but instead of healing that wound, she turned the shame she felt into money shame because she felt unworthy of the money that was rightfully hers. Your story may be less dramatic, but I'm asking you to suss out the shards of shame hidden in your story. To heal the pain, you have to first feel it.

SELF-DIRECTION #3: Uncover Your Money Shame

Consider completing the next exercise with a trusted, skilled support person. Uncover your shame by going deeper into your money story. Begin by asking yourself to recall a time when you:

- Felt worthless because of money

- Felt stupid because of money

- Felt selfish because of money

- Felt inadequate because of money

- Used money to belong

Write about one or more of these times in your money journal. As you do this, don't worry for now about the reasons behind your shame. Don't get caught up in analyzing your story! There will be time for that later in the money detox. For now, just tell your story. Here are some questions to help you focus:

- Where in your body do you feel shame?

- How can you best describe your feeling of shame?

- Who (if anyone) is with you when you feel shame?

- What makes your shame feel worse?

- What do you do when you feel shame?

4

Identify Your Money Beliefs

The mind is a powerful tool. The moment you change your perception is the moment you rewrite the chemistry of your body.

— Dr. Bruce H. Lipton

Because I was trapped in my circle of money pain for so long, I know what it feels like to be in that financial suffering grind. I understand how the mind can take you in all these different directions related to shame and finances. You wake up in the morning, and the first thing you think about is money. You check your bank account. You might worry about how you will pay your bills. You might worry about your investments. It doesn't matter where you are on the spectrum, how much money you do or don't have, fear attacks you daily. This money neurosis isn't limited to your waking moments, either. It invades your thoughts both night and day, in both your conscious and subconscious minds.

And, of course, you can't tell anybody about the shame and fear you're experiencing. That would be too horrific!

The only way to get a handle on toxic money shame is to grab it by the roots and pull it up. For that, you have to know what the roots are, and where in you they are growing. It also helps to know their origins in specific moments of your life. In this chapter, I will guide you to identify the money beliefs that are at the root of your shame, and that keep the circle of money pain in motion.

Let's start with a simple exercise.

SELF-DIRECTION #4: Your Money Words

Words have a lot of power. All it takes is somebody to curse you out for that to become apparent. Sometimes it's only a single word.

Here, I'm asking you to do something called *free association*. When you free associate, you are given a trigger word or idea, and then you see what words come to your mind. The key is to do this without thinking about the trigger or the words, and without censoring anything. Just say the first words that come to mind.

The trigger here is the word MONEY.

Hold the word money in your mind. Then write down in your money journal whatever words come to your mind. You can do this for a few minutes. Don't do it for too long, or you'll get in your head and start thinking about it.

Consider exploring the word MONEY in relation to all the dimensions of your life, such as family, friends, community, home, entertainment, vacations, spirituality, work, health, and pets.

Looking at Your Money Belief Legacy

If you look at the words you free associated with *money*, you'll probably have a pretty good idea about the kind of money beliefs that drive your life.

To be clear, I'm not suggesting that all money beliefs are negative or bad or to be eliminated. Take a minute and review the words you just free associated. Are they primarily positive or negative? Or a mixture of both? Where it gets tricky is that money words and money beliefs can sometimes sound positive when in reality, they are the roots of toxic shame.

The money belief I heard all the time from my mother was, "If only we had money, then everything would be better." This mantra was as constant as the North star—a faraway, beckoning, twinkling light in the sky that continually reminded us that if not for the lack of money, then life could and would be perfect. I grew up conscious of my mother's obsession with the cost of every single thing, which resulted in right-down-to-the-penny living. This world of needs and wants and dollars was a puzzle we couldn't manage to solve. Despite our circumstances, and true to my mother's shame pattern, we looked good. My brothers and I were the best-dressed kids in school, and we won awards to prove it.

While my mother didn't hug us or kiss us or tell us she

loved us, she bought us things. She was logical and practical and believed you had to save for a rainy day, yet she spent her extra pennies on clothes and sugar. Clothes made you look good, and sugar made you feel good. My best childhood memories are the times we went shopping together, especially walking to Lil Peach convenience store to get Hostess cupcakes and other bakery items. Sugar was how we numbed the idea that if only we had money, then everything would be okay. My aunts and uncles stepped up to help because they knew my father had run out on my mother. Looking back, we were pretty fortunate that we had so many adults in our lives. But that wasn't enough to break the cycle, that crushing circle of money pain.

On the surface, the money belief that "money will make everything better" can sound positive. It creates the sense of money as the great savior. Who wouldn't want that? It's only when we look at the whole picture, and see how that belief can be at the root of so much toxic shame, that its true negative power is apparent.

A key step in chipping away at my family's legacy was identifying the messages about money I heard as a kid. These words were so ingrained in me that I didn't even notice their impact until my brother shot himself with a crossbow to get out of his loop of money shame and debt:

"If only we had money, everything would be okay."

"You have to look good."

"Work hard."

"Work is your worth."

"Money is your value."

"Save for a rainy day."

The best way to identify these messages is to begin telling your story and having conversations with family members. When clients come to see me for coaching, I tell them, "If you don't have conversations about money with somebody, let me tell you what can happen. Let me tell you what happened to me."

Our money beliefs come to us in a variety of ways and through a variety of sources, including our social and work environments. However, the money beliefs that hold the greatest sway over us—for good or for bad—tend to be the ones we acquired in our family while growing up. Our parents' and grandparents' beliefs shaped our beliefs at a time when our young minds were wide open and our personalities were just developing. For this reason, digging up the roots of your money beliefs involves recalling what the influential people in your early life thought about and did with money.

The next exercise will help you identify these inherited money beliefs.

SELF-DIRECTION #5: Your Inherited Money Beliefs

Answer the following questions in your money journal. I have listed your mother and father, but go ahead and add or substitute other influential people: grandparents, aunts, uncles, stepparents, caregivers, and so on.

Mother:

My mother's main money belief was: _____

My mother used money to: _____

I learned from mother that money: _____

My mother's reaction to money was: _____

Father:

My father's main money belief was: _____

My father used money to: _____

I learned from father that money: _____

My father's reaction to money was: _____

Your Legacy Doesn't Determine Your Future

Once you have identified your inherited money beliefs, there are several things you can do next to further the money detox process. Remember, your legacy doesn't have to determine your future, unless you decide that that's what you want.

First, consider whether you have adopted any of these beliefs yourself. Be honest about it. For example, if your father always said money was the root of evil, did you come away believing that, too? Even if you don't want to admit it to yourself, is that what you believe deep down?

As you consider the degree to which you have inherited the money beliefs you identified, pay attention to what you wrote both about your parents' (or other influencers') beliefs as well as actions, and how those beliefs and actions were related. Your mother, for example, might have said that money is a force for good, but you never saw her give a dime to charity. In this case, which message had the most powerful and lasting influence on your own beliefs?

First, you can start to more clearly articulate your own money beliefs; that is, starting with the money beliefs you inherited. Write them down in your money journal.

Second, consider the quality of your parents' (or other influencers') money beliefs. This is where you ask yourself: is this a positive or negative legacy? Determine whether you are happy with the influence or whether it is something you want to change asap.

Here are some examples of positive money beliefs:

- I am worth the amount of money I am capable of spending.
- Money is love, I receive as much as I give.
- Money is currency circulation; give and I shall receive.
- Money is good, use it for good. Money buys freedom of choice.

Here are some examples of negative money beliefs:

- My self-worth is equal to my net worth, my home, my car, my credit score, my job.
- More money will make me happy.
- Money is the root of all evil.
- I don't deserve money when others have so little.

As you think about the negative and positive qualities of the money beliefs in your legacy, consider how they relate to money shame. Look again at the money shame stories you uncovered in the previous chapter. At that point, you were focused on feelings and gut impact. Now is the time to return to those feelings and see which, if any, are based on the money beliefs in your legacy.

Recall Jean, the woman who didn't claim her pension because she was too ashamed after she cheated on her husband? I didn't go into detail about the money beliefs she uncovered during her money detox, but here are some common beliefs that fit her situation:

- You have to earn every penny of your wealth.
- If you do bad things, God will punish you by taking away what you earned.
- Bad people don't deserve any rewards in life.
- You must pay for your sins.

Stephanie's Story

Stephanie sat on the couch in my office, nearly in tears. "My husband is just burning through our money, and I can't stop him. He's blowing thousands and thousands of dollars every month on everything you can imagine! He refuses to get help. What can I do to help myself and stay married?"

Stephanie was a local entrepreneur, the third generation in a family of hard workers and innovators. Her net worth was quite substantial. However, she was miserable. She and her husband had been married for over twenty years, which meant she'd had a lot of time to develop anger and resentment over the way he spent their money.

The truth was that Stephanie was a *financial enabler*. Because she was terrified of disappointing her husband, she could not set healthy boundaries with him. She was frozen by her shame. So instead of trying to work out her ever-increasing dissatisfaction, she said nothing. While some of their big-ticket purchases (can you say "European vacations"?) took the sting out of her resentment for a few moments, generally, the excessive spending was part and parcel of their dysfunctional lifestyle.

Stephanie was a victim of the circumstances of her own making, and lived in a continual state of profound scarcity. While we can all have a scarcity mindset from time to time, in my experience, it appears to be deeper and more prominent among the wealthy. I believe this is in large part due to the inherited money beliefs from their Depression-era parents and grandparents.

Most of the wealth in the world is passed down from one generation to another, causing enormous amounts of pressure on the adult children to spend wisely and pass it on to their children or a charity. According to a 2015 article in *Time* magazine: "Indeed, 70% of wealthy families lose their wealth by the second generation, and a stunning 90% by the third, according to the Williams Group wealth consultancy."[1] Talk about pressure!

Stephanie was not a good steward of her money, and she knew it and felt a paralyzing sense of shame. Her shame and fear were so ingrained that she had to blame her husband;

1. Chris Taylor, "70% of Rich Families Lose Their Wealth by the Second Generation," *Money* (June 17, 2015), time.com/money/3925308/rich-families-lose-wealth/.

she could not take responsibility for her part at all. Eventually, she admitted to me that she was spending as much as he was on the kind of luxuries her father would never have considered buying. The idea of her father knowing about her spending habits was hugely shame inducing. It didn't matter that her father was no longer alive.

With that admission, I was able to help Stephanie uncover her toxic shame. We then dug up its roots and identified her limiting money beliefs.

When I talked to Stephanie about her money beliefs, I used the term *money scripts*. I said, "Money scripts are the messages you received as a kid, mostly from your family. They form your money beliefs. What money scripts did you hear your mother and father say?"

Stephanie said, "My mom was a dancer and didn't talk about money."

"So no actual script from her?"

"No. But I guess the message I received was 'Money isn't something we talk about.'"

I nodded. "Right. And your father?"

"He was a businessman and handled the family's money. He often said, 'Stephanie, we have to work hard to make money, so don't be foolish and wasteful. Be smart and save for the future.' I heard that message loud and clear. Which is why I now feel like I'm disrespecting my father. I should know better."

"That makes perfect sense," I said. "No wonder this is so painful for you."

Her father's money beliefs were such a large part of Stephanie's beliefs that she hadn't even recognized they were inherited and not her own. The money belief of "Don't be foolish with your money" played in her mind all day every day as she watched herself and her husband do just that.

A budget was not going to fix Stephanie's situation, just like with my brother Keith. Instead, for many months, we worked on her resentments, grievances, self-forgiveness, and self-compassion. I worked closely with her to rewrite her money beliefs. Under my guidance, Stephanie realized that her husband did not have to change for her to live a happy life. She didn't have to leave her marriage either; she just had to accept him for exactly who he was and set healthy boundaries. For her part, Stephanie was trusting and willing to do the work to master her emotions—specifically shame and fear—and shift her inherited money beliefs. Stephanie and her husband are soon to celebrate their twenty-fifth wedding anniversary, and she smiles a lot more.

The Scarcity Mindset

One common money belief can be summed up as the *scarcity mindset*, or the belief that there isn't enough to go around. Lynne Twist, a cofounder of The Pachamama Alliance and founder of The Soul of Money Institute, wrote *The Soul of Money*, in which she focuses on the concept of scarcity.[2]

One of the most significant stories in her book, for me, was about Mother Teresa. Lynne Twist is Catholic, and her dream was to meet Mother Teresa, so she went to Mother Teresa's Indian orphanage, where she had a profound experience. She witnessed a wealthy husband and wife mistreat Mother Teresa. After Lynne returned to the states, Mother Teresa sent her a letter that read, "The wealthy suffer deeply, and we judge them so harshly. They hide behind closed doors and don't feel safe to share who they are because they can't trust that we will accept them for their authentic selves. Most people hang out with wealthy people to be in the special, powerful group, not because they authentically like the people."

Mother Teresa's letter changed the direction of my consciousness. I started seeing wealthy people differently. I recognized that they, too, can be "poor" and in need of support. Mother Teresa often spoke about the scarcity

2. Lynne Twist, *The Soul of Money: Reclaiming the Wealth of Our Inner Resources* (New York: W.W. Norton, 2006).

mindset prevalent in America. People live with a scarcity mindset because they believe they don't have enough.

Think about what happens when we get a severe weather warning. In the South, we get warnings about hurricanes coming to wipe us out. We stock up. But we don't just take what we need, we buy more, more, more—which creates the energy of scarcity and leads to clutter and hoarding. All out of fear. Hoarding is driven by the fear that we're going to lose something we have or that we're not going to get something we need.

Lynne Twist lists three money myths that define the scarcity mindset.[3]

The first myth is "There's not enough." This creates a subconscious mindset that sets our expectations for what is possible. When we wake up in the morning, our first thought is what will project us forward. The first thing I used to do after I woke up in the morning was look at my bank account. Immediately, I was filled with anxiety and worry about money. I lived all day with a scarcity mindset.

Now when I wake up, I say, "Thank you." I immediately counter any expectations of scarcity with gratitude.

Many people don't know they have a scarcity mindset. They don't realize they're living in it to the degree that they are. The scarcity mindset that believes "There's not enough" can take many forms:

3. Lynne Twist, *The Soul of Money*.

- I don't have enough time.

- I don't have enough money.

- If others get what they want, there won't be enough left for me.

- If I give to others, I won't have enough left for me.

The second myth is "More is better." This addresses our need to accumulate. Think about how the storage unit business cropped up in the 1970s, and how it has since grown into a billion-dollar industry. We have containers of stuff that we must store elsewhere because we can't fit it into our homes. That's a scarcity mentality! We're hoarding everywhere. Not to mention that the amount we pay to store that stuff over time sooner or later becomes greater than its actual value.

We're inundated with messages from the media and from advertising that bigger is better, more is better. For a while, the fast-food industry promoted the biggie size and the supersize to make customers think they were getting more. We went from small neighborhood stores to Costco and Sam's and Super Walmart and Super Target. Cosmetics promoted longer and thicker lashes and fuller lips and bigger butts and longer, thicker hair. We've gotten sicker and sicker because of all this stuff, and you can see that across every socio-economic level in our culture. Billionaires go from a small boat to a massive yacht, from a three-thousand-square-foot house to a mansion, from one car to fifteen cars, with garages to match. It's not just that the Joneses are doing it, but the billionaires are doing it, as well.

The third myth is "That's just the way it is." This addresses the culture of shame and powerlessness. If you think, "That's just the way it is," then there is nothing you can do to change. You are stuck in powerlessness and shame.

People who come to me with so much shame and the mindset that they can't do anything about it are caught in the clutches of these three myths. My job is to get them out of the scarcity mindset so they can feel whole again and choose healthy money beliefs.

The money detox process isn't a quick fix. It's a slow wake-up. Pray for patience because when you want to live a conscious life, it doesn't happen overnight. We have to peel back a lot of layers to heal.

Clutter and Hoarding

In my coaching practice, I see clutter of every type, shape, and substance you can imagine. I see emotional clutter and physical clutter. Much of that clutter is related to grief and shame, which is related to the fear of scarcity, fear of not having enough. Clutter is evidence of an unhealthy financial mindset.

UCLA researchers Darby Saxbe and Rena Repetti found that clutter correlates with mood, and especially depression, as well as with levels of cortisol—the body's main stress hormone.[4]

I didn't know how much clutter I had until I moved from a 2,800-square-feet house to one that was only 1,100 square feet, which forced me to clean out my closets. All my clothes and shoes had been spread across three closets, so I hadn't seen everything at once. When I pulled out all the shoes and started counting, I had 222 pairs! At least twenty percent of those pairs had never been worn. I saw that this accumulation was the result of grief. A relationship ended, and I went shopping. I felt sad or lonely, and I went shopping. Those overstuffed closets were the undeniable evidence of my unaddressed grief.

When you amass clutter, you have to ask, "What can it teach me? What does it tell me about my money beliefs?"

When you start to get curious about why you stockpile, you will see how it connects with toxic money shame and the underlying money belief "I'm not enough." The intention is to get to "I am enough," and the automatic impulse is to accumulate and to hoard. Of course, accumulating extra stuff will never achieve that result.

---

4. Darby E. Saxbe and Rena Repetti, "No Place Like Home: Home Tours Correlate With Daily Patterns of Mood and Cortisol," *Personality and Social Psychology Bulletin* 36, no. 1 (2009):71–81.

To take it to a deeper level, clutter is a physical manifestation of not letting go of the past, of not working through emotions from the past—whether the past represents grief, shame, fear, or something else we're clinging to. Grief is a constant in our lives—we lose loved ones, we lose relationships, we lose jobs, we lose friendships, we lose the childhood we wish we had. Feeling that grief is part of healing, but the next element in healing is letting go of the grief and letting go of the past.

Too often we don't address and heal our pain; we move on to the next thing to numb ourselves. We live in a numbing culture. We don't like pain, and we want to replace it as quickly as possible with the next happy thing. We're in pursuit of happiness, and we pursue it through what is available to us in the external material world.

The kind of happiness that generates is temporary and fleeting because it depends on something outside yourself. Joy, on the other hand, is found within yourself. It is independent of external circumstances, and it brings a lot more satisfaction. Happiness is easy: just go to the store and buy a pair of shoes, and you're happy. For a moment. To sustain joy is an inside job. That's where you meet your soul.

I am here to show you how to find your power and strength and stop feeling so powerless over money. Stop giving money so much power. Give up your scarcity mindset. Even if you're a minimalist, you could be hoarding email. You could be hoarding data. Once you stop and take a look at what you like to accumulate, you might be shocked at what you find.

SELF-DIRECTION #6: Clean House

Unless you are a minimalist, this exercise is for you. It's time to take stock of what you'd like to let go.

1. In case you are ambivalent about letting go, let's start with simply seeing what you have. Pick a room in your house. It could be your office space, your kitchen, your garage, your attic—wherever you want to look first.

2. Take inventory of what you have in this space. You can do it by writing up a list. Or you can take photos of the stuff with your phone. Either way, get in there and lay everything out so you can get a good look at it.

3. Now go through all the items and ask yourself some questions (these are just suggested questions; feel free to come up with your own):

- How long since I last used this?

- Does this belong to me or should it be returned to its owner?

- Could someone else make better use of this?

- Is this broken, smell bad, or belong in the trash?

- Would I feel liberated without this item?

4. Acknowledge what you are ready to let go of. It helps to

have destination for each item you have decided to let go
(the trash, a friend, a charity).

5. Now it's time take this exercise up a notch. If you really
want to live the life of your dreams, you have to become
willing to clean house, to let go of the past and maintain
that. This includes your finances, your body, and all the
spaces you live in.

This is a tall order and might cause major discomfort.
Take it slowly. Complete all of the following over the next
year. Ask for help. You may want to engage with a money
coach.

- Clean your house from top to bottom.

- Get your office or place of work clean and organized.

- Get your car clean and organized and keep it that way.

- Get up to date on all correspondence.

- Get rid of or fix anything that doesn't work.

- Return what's been borrowed or make an agreement
  with its owner.

- Get back what's been lent or make an agreement about
  it.

- Balance your checkbook and keep it balanced.

- Pay all you bills on time or make arrangements in
  advance.

- If any bill is past due, make an arrangement or agreement to pay it.

- Organize all personal records and files.

- Keep tax information up to date.

- Get your body in shape and keep it that way.

As you do this deep cleaning, your life will be filled with blessings.

Marie-Helena's Story

Marie-Helena came to me with the goal of unwinding a lifetime of scarcity consciousness so she could experience faith in abundance. Early in our coaching relationship, she shared a story with me that perfectly illustrates the perils of scarcity and poverty mindsets.

Once when she was on a budget vacation, she had to use a public laundromat, which required getting bills to put into the change machine in order to get quarters. While she was loading her clothes into the washer, she noticed a quarter on top of the washer next to the one she was using. She knew it was not hers. Furthermore, since this was a low-income area, she knew whoever put it there most certainly needed it more than she did. However, she couldn't help herself. She took it and added it to her collection of quarters. She said she felt like she had "scored."

When it came time to move her clothes to a dryer, Marie-Helena loaded her clothes into one and inserted two quarters. However, then she noticed that she had put the quarters into the slot for the dryer above the one where her clothes were. That dryer was already running—with someone else's laundry. Oops! Fifty cents lost right off the bat.

So Marie-Helena put quarters into the correct slot and sat down to wait for the load to dry.

As she watched the laundry circling, she began to feel bad. Although she had only taken one quarter, she couldn't shake the guilt that came from lifting something that wasn't hers. She also realized why she had done it: her scarcity mindset told her that one quarter made a big difference to her.

Marie-Helena was ready to let go of the scarcity mindset. She took all her remaining quarters (which totalled one dollar) and set them on the washer where she had taken the quarter. She knew it was not a given that the same person would get that dollar, but she looked upon it as her gift to the universe.

When her load was finished, it was not all dry. But she had no more quarters. So she carried her damp clothes back to her room and hung them in the bathroom to finish drying.

Taking that one quarter had cost her $1.50 and resulted in a major inconvenience. But it had also taught her a valuable lesson. If we could all learn to let go of our scarcity mindsets for a buck-fifty, what a bargain that would be!

The Spiritual Bypass

A scarcity mindset is relatively straightforward: you believe that you won't have enough. But I have run across various permutations of this mindset that are much harder to sort out. In one convoluted version, people convince themselves that they are entitled to what amounts to an overabundance. I see this most often when people have a money belief they view as religiously or spiritually based. They may buy into the notion that if they give money to the church or to a religious organization or even a nonprofit, they will automatically prosper. They tell themselves that God will take care of them, no matter what. At the core of this belief, however, is a scarcity mindset that centers on assumptions that sound something like "I have nothing but what God gives me."

Some versions of this belief turn into what is known as a *spiritual bypass*; that is, a spiritual notion that is appropriated to avoid being genuinely spiritual. In practice, believing that the universe owes us something in return for our good behavior is not so different from expecting to win the lottery simply because we believe in abundance.

Naturally, I am a believer in tithing, but it must be reasonable and done responsibly. Tithing should not put an individual or family in hardship. When people act out of what they consider a spiritual belief, then it can be almost impossible to counter that belief. After all, they are already being spiritual, right? In their eyes, they are already on the right side of God. Their belief closes them off to their inner wisdom and precludes the willingness to let go of old money beliefs that is necessary for a successful money detox. This can lead to a massive disappointment, even ruin. Consider what happened to Denny.

Denny's Story

As soon as Denny walked into my office, I could see he was a magnet for disaster. He was full of anger, resentment, and debt, and he informed me he was facing foreclosure, bankruptcy, and a host of other lawsuits. He was burning through hundreds of thousands of dollars, while running scared and obsessing about what the world was doing to him. Because he was in some form of upset all the time, I realized he needed more help than I could provide, and decided it would best to involve a team of colleagues.

After a few months of working together, things started to settle down. Nevertheless, Denny remained unwilling to work through a money detox. He would address neither his shame nor his money beliefs. Instead, he clung to the belief, "If I am good, then everything will be taken care of." In my experience, that is one of the hardest money beliefs to deal with.

Toward the end of our time together, Denny received a large, long overdue financial settlement. Although he needed every bit of that money to pay for his home and living expenses, take care of his children, and pay off many unpaid debts, he decided to give almost all of it to the church.

Our team was astounded. We watched as he struggled to make ends meet, at a time when he should have finally had financial security. He continued to face foreclosure, putting undue and unnecessary stress on others to rescue his family. Unfortunately, I have to report that things did not end well for Denny.

5

Discover Your Worth

Marianne Williamson's book *A Return to Love* shifted my perception of everything in my life when I read it.[1] She said there are only two emotions: love and fear. In the introduction, she says, "The spiritual journey is the relinquishment or unlearning of fear and the acceptance of love back into our hearts. Love is the essential, existential fact. It is our ultimate reality and our purpose on Earth. To be consciously aware of it, to experience love in ourselves and others is the meaning of life."

She brings money into it when she says, "Meaning doesn't lie in things. Meaning lies in us. When we attach value to things that aren't love—the money, the cars, the

1. Marianne Williamson, *A Return to Love: Reflections on the Principles of a Course in Miracles* (San Francisco: HarperOne, 1996).

house, the prestige—we are loving things that can't love us back. We are searching for meaning in the meaningless. Money, of itself, means nothing. Materials things, of themselves, mean nothing. It's not that they're bad. It's that they are nothing."

We tend to look for love in all the wrong places, like spending money to feel love. This is a dangerous form of fantasy, of addiction. After Keith's death, I could no longer deny that something was terribly, terribly wrong in my family. I slowly began to wake up from decades of sleep. Once awake, I was confronted with the painful truth of what I had valued most and where I had placed my worth. I had allowed fear to drive me, not love. Those were harsh realities to face, but it had to be done if I wanted to be financially successful.

As I investigated my own story more deeply and faced my fears, I discovered that I'd always had a knowing about love inside, even if I felt I'd lost my way. I saw that we have to become willing to surrender to get back to our roots. We have to choose love over fear.

Curiosity and Grit

If we don't go deeply into our stories—if we don't get curious about ourselves, about our behavior, about our thinking, and about our circumstances—then shame can kill us. How? We will suffocate under debt. We will die addicted. Like my brother, we may take our lives when the pain of it all becomes too much to bear. Becoming curious and having the courage to ask questions and find another way is one means of displaying grit. If you don't disrupt the cycle and do something new or different, then you're going to keep shaming. I want to show you, and assure you, that there's a way out of this shame. I want you to see that you have the ability to take a new path, one that is driven by love not fear, one in which you know your own true worth.

Even at a young age, I wanted answers to my many questions.

When we were living in Westford, I would visit other families in our neighborhood, such as the Sullivans next door. I sensed I could get a perspective there that I couldn't get at home. Mrs. Sullivan was a Harvard graduate, and Mr. Sullivan was an MIT graduate, which made them fascinating to me. I loved to ask them questions because they had answers. They had lives and interests and stories and livelihoods.

I visited my father's mother, Helen, as often as I could, as she provided another type of stimulation I craved. She was an educator, and I believe she enjoyed teaching me as much as I enjoyed learning. She taught me how to fish and how to cut the grass and how to take care of a dog. There was so much to learn!

At a young age, I became conscious of the difference between my home and the homes of these two women, and

I saw what I wanted for myself and what I didn't want. I learned such a variety of different things from Mrs. Sullivan and my grandmother Helen. Still, even after visiting them, I would go back to my mother's house and sink right back into the toxic deadness inside.

When I was older, babysitting for neighborhood families allowed me to earn my own money to buy some of the personal items I wanted, such as clothes and record albums, and the things young teens need. My mother hadn't taught me the basic things I needed to know about being a female. She told me I was going to have a period, but that was about all she said. I had to learn the whole maintenance part through trial and error. When I became a teenager, I needed help with simple things, such as grooming. But my mother didn't have it in her to help me—neither the time, nor the interest, nor the money. So I babysat to earn my own money to pay for what I needed.

When we moved to Maryland, we had neighbors who were in the restaurant business, and I went to school with their daughters. No doubt recognizing my need for personal attention, they invited me along with them to their hairdresser rather than let me get my standard $10 haircut.

This was my first experience at a cool salon with fancy hair stylists, and I saw what people with a little bit of money could afford. There, I met a stylist named Susan. She was about eight or ten years older than me, and she took an immediate liking to me. She said, "When you're old enough, I'm going to get you a job. Come back when you turn fifteen, and you can start working here. But in the meantime, we're going to clean up your hair and your eyebrows." I had big eyebrows, and unruly hair that refused to behave. Finally, someone could see me and see what I needed!

Susan ended up becoming my first mentor. I went to work part time at the salon when I turned fifteen and stayed all the way through high school. In the beginning, I worked as a shampoo girl, and I kept that place spick and span, top to bottom. The owners and employees used to remark on my work ethic, saying I was the best worker they'd ever had. They loved me and took me in as a part of the family. They became big influencers in my life and gave me the opportunity to see a small business up close and personal. I worked my way up from shampoo girl to cashier to manager of the front desk, and then I started doing the books with one of the owners at night. Working at the salon taught me a lot about managing money, products, and profit margins.

That was my first job with a small business. I also worked for the government when I was in high school. I was on a work-release program from school, and they placed me with the government. I hated that damn job. There was nothing about the government that was interesting to me. It was as flat and uninteresting as my home. It was very structured, and nobody did any work. I was a fitness fanatic by then, and at that office, everybody was obese and had parties nearly every day, with cakes and pies and luncheons. I had a three-month job, yet I did all the work they had for me in the first two weeks. They didn't know what to do with me and my work ethic.

I had another job on the side because I was always interested in trying new things. I went to work for a health club, where I learned how to sell. All the jobs I had were big influencers, gifting me with many lessons in each position as I went along. I was exposed to Tony Robbins, Zig Ziglar, and Brian Tracy—a lot of the prominent sales people in the eighties. I got into fitness and meditation and had many cool experiences. It all went back to being curious and having a willingness to be open to learning.

You won't develop curiosity or grit, however, if you are confident that blind luck will reward you instead. In my mother's family, most played the lottery. And they won. My uncle won a million bucks in the eighties. My aunt won millions, as well. Even my mother got a few nice wins: $10,000 and $20,000. The overwhelming way of thinking about retirement in my family is *I need to hit the numbers. Everything will be fine then.*

Of course, it's nice to hit the lottery, and a lottery mindset is hard to escape when some people in your family have been fortunate to have such good luck. The problem in my family came from thinking all they had to do was wait for that next big hit, which was never a sure thing. Because, after all, despite some of my family members' extraordinary luck, you have as much chance of winning the lottery as, well, winning the lottery.

Curiosity and grit can carry you far. But these qualities have to be based on a set of sound values and on an understanding of your true self-worth. Otherwise, your curiosity will be limited to wondering about the winning lottery number or the price of your neighbor's new car. Your grit will be no more than a grin-and-bear-it stance, as you pray no one finds out about your latest financial screw up.

Often it takes a crisis or hitting rock bottom to realize what really matters to us. Preferably, though, no one has to die and you don't have to suffer even more before you are able to identify your true worth. This element of the money detox asks you to examine your values. As when you were examining your inherited beliefs, don't make judgments about yourself or your values. Follow your curiosity and let it reveal what is important to you. If you don't like what you discover, there will be time later to work at revising your value structure.

SELF-DIRECTION #7: What is important to me?

Imagine you have just won the lottery. Your entire life, as you have known it, is about to change forever. Answer the following questions as honestly as you can. Remember there are no right or wrong answers.

1. How much is your lottery ticket worth?
2. How does having all that money make you feel?
3. Would you prefer people know or not know of your newly acquired wealth? Why?
4. In what way(s) will the quality of your life be affected by winning, for good and/or for bad?
5. What are you going to do with the money? Make a specific plan. How much money will you give yourself per month? Who will share in the winnings? Write everything down step by step.
6. What aspects of your plan are essential to your happiness?

My Many Cars

I love cars. Cars were one way my struggle to clarify my true worth played out over the years.

I bought my first car when I was seventeen. It was a black two-door Mustang LX with a sunroof. When I drove off the lot, I suddenly felt absolute and total freedom. I had a way out of the house, to drive to work, to explore, and to see the world around me.

In high school, I had carpooled to a private all-girls school where most of the girls were either from middle- or upper-class white-collar families or from military/government families. My family was decidedly blue-collar, and I didn't invite anyone over because we didn't have a beautiful house. Peter drove a work pickup truck, and my mom had an older Pontiac that somehow survived three teenage drivers. I was dissatisfied with everything at home. Since homes and cars were how we categorized and judged our neighbors, both were a place of brutal shame for me.

As soon as I bought that Mustang, I drove around wealthy neighborhoods and dreamed of a happier life and nicer things. Sometimes I took myself to expensive restaurants, such as The Palm, where I once ordered a four-pound lobster for $100 just because I could. I hadn't grown up with the luxury of eating out or taking vacations. Our family went to Sizzler on special occasions, and our holidays tended to be at local beaches or national parks.

I started dressing a certain way, changing my style to a more classic yuppie fashion. I shopped at the local Casual Corner and Hecht department store, which felt like a massive jump up from Filene's Basement, a discount clothing store where we shopped as children. I wanted to play in a different world. I had a champagne taste with a beer budget, but that didn't stop me. I received my first American Express credit card in the mail when I turned eighteen. I felt like a real bigshot.

As I made more money, I upgraded my car accordingly, because I wanted everyone to think I was successful and worthy of love and belonging. I desperately wanted to fit in the way that little girl standing out in the cold in Alicia's driveway never did. I moved across the river from suburban Maryland to Virginia, where I took a sales job. I rose quickly up the ladder and traded the Mustang for a Honda. That felt more in alignment with the white-collar middle-class world where I wanted to live.

However, as soon as the new-car smell had worn off, I felt like I had arrived and it was time to upgrade. I visited my first Mercedes dealer. The white male salesman wanted to know if I had a husband, and asked if I could afford a Mercedes. I was offended as I was working my ass off, earning over $100,000. I left that dealership and went to another, where I was treated as an equal by an Iranian man.

We were friends for years to come. I made a point of returning to the first dealership after I purchased my brand-new Benz so I could give the sales manager my two cents about discriminating against women.

As good as I felt in the Benz, my car-buying rigamarole was the beginning of another level of spending to cover up my shame. When I was driving a Mercedes, people treated me with more respect. They were more curious about me. They wanted to know what I did for a living and how was I so successful. This type of interaction fed into my low self-esteem and kept me holding onto the car, as well as all the other material trappings, even when the facts and figures screamed that I should be selling them.

Soon after I bought that Mercedes, I moved to Florida, where I owned a home with a Mercedes on one side of the driveway and a BMW on the other side, a white picket fence, two dogs, and a girlfriend. I had indeed arrived. We had looking good down cold.

I landed a job as a medical device sales rep, which I enjoyed because I got to wine and dine my doctor clients at fancy restaurants. The job had its perks, and I got a company car. However, my girlfriend and I broke up, so although I had the company car and didn't have any debts, and my mortgage was very reasonable, I was suffering. I figured a Porsche convertible would cure my loneliness. And it did. For a few minutes. As I pulled out of the dealership in my new silver Porsche convertible, with a red interior, I felt alive, full, satisfied, and successful.

When I got home and opened the garage door, I realized my two-car garage was already full. And I was single. I panicked, knowing I'd made a big mistake. I could have returned the car to the dealership, as there is a three-day right of rescission when you purchase a new car in Florida. That didn't occur to me, though. Numbing did. I went inside and poured a glass of wine to numb the pain.

It took many more years for me to recognize that my pattern of purchasing cars was closely attached to my money shame, not measuring up, keeping up with the Joneses, and looking for love in all the wrong places. Buying cars was a clear indicator of the depth of disconnection between myself and the God of my understanding.

One day, after I was well into my money detox, I was driving through my upper-class neighborhood, full of really nice cars, and I had the brilliant idea to test drive a Range Rover Sport. However, at the point, I knew what was behind my desire. So instead of rushing to the dealership, I went home and called my 12-step sponsor and had a good cry. I was merely feeling sad and lonely.

When the wish for a Rover returned a week later, I decided to approach it as a research project. With my emotions in check, I looked at the value of my current car and compared it with the accompanying costs of a new Rover, including the increased insurance cost, the costly

SUV collision insurance, the repair cost, and the gas cost. Once I had completed my analysis, it was clear the purchase would not be in alignment with my priorities and values at the time, nor with my budget. Then I called the dealership and scheduled a test drive. Because I love cars. After the test drive, I thanked them and went on my merry way.

Today I'm still driving my 2012 Acura sports wagon, with over 100,000 miles. Better yet, it's all paid off! Am I happy driving this car? Yes. Because I am clear about what is important to me and how I want to spend my money. However, clarifying your money values doesn't always mean spending less. It can mean spending more. Consider Jill's story.

Jill's Story

Jill and I met at her home for her first money coaching session. Her house was quite large but sparsely furnished, as if she had just moved in. During our conversation, I learned that Jill retired at the age of fifty-five, with a pension and four million dollars in savings. Quite an accomplishment, considering that her highest annual income had been $45,000. She really knew the power of living beneath her means.

I asked her how she did it.

"I took full advantage of my company's stock purchase plan by learning how to maximize it. I didn't spend money on things, just the basics. I have a ten-year-old car, very minimal clothes, and a chair and TV. That's about it." Jill was very proud of her minimalist life.

But there was a catch. She had recently begun dating a woman named Bonnie, who had quite the opposite lifestyle: very materialistic, with lots of clothes, shoes, a big house. She had millions of dollars saved for retirement, as well.

Jill told me she wanted to be free, to start to spend her money, to travel and buy new clothes. But she couldn't let herself do it.

She and Bonnie were getting into arguments over lifestyle and finances. Jill told Bonnie, "Your spending is reckless. You're going to run out of money."

After many arguments, Jill recognized that her minimalist life style was not a conscious choice but came more out of feeling, "I am not worthy to have stuff. I have to be responsible, save, and get by with the basics." That set of values was holding her back from living a wholehearted life.

As she went through the money detox, Jill became willing to judge herself less and accept herself more, as well as to do the same for Bonnie. She eased up on her money control, and they still lived easily within their budget. Within a year, they had gotten married and were traveling the world. They bought a big new home together and filled each room with treasures from their travels.

The next exercise is similar to the fantasy lottery exercise you just did, but this time you are going to look at your actual use of money.

SELF-DIRECTION #8: The Money Challenge

Challenge One: Begin by learning where your money is going. Follow your dollars for the next seven days. I know how challenging it can be to look closely at your spending for one day, so if you can do it for seven days, that will be a big success. "Follow your dollars" means tracking all of your daily spending. Write it down in your money journal by category. I suggest you do this with pen and paper, not just on your cell phone. Your brain needs a shift.

Challenge Two: Go into your bank accounts and see exactly where your money goes. See each line item as evidence of what you value. Categorizes your spending (dining out, pets, entertainment, groceries , beauty, clothes, travel, iTunes, Amazon). Then ask yourself:

- What surprises me about my spending?
- Does my spending reflect what I value?
- What shifts can I make to bring my spending into alignment with my values?

We spend money on what we make a priority in our life. Often, our priorities are not in alignment with what we truly value, which you may notice as you do this exercise. So why do we do this? We simply don't look closely at where our money goes.

Being out of integrity with your values can cause an internal unrest that leaves you wondering what is wrong with you. You wonder, "Why do I feel so anxious and worried about money most of the time?" When your spending priorities are not in sync with your values, you create an internal conflict of fear, shame, worry, and anxiety. Are you ready to give up this turmoil? By following your dollars, you can make a shift into freedom today.

Marcus's Story

Marcus's story shows the importance of appreciating one's self-worth. Although he was trained at one of the best culinary schools in the country, Marcus worked as a chef at a middle-level restaurant, where his pay check wasn't enough to cover all the things his family needed. Marcus was a black man and he was married to a white woman, who was an interior designer. They had three children and lived in a wealthy white neighborhood in the Northeast. Marcus's in-laws were wealthy and had been helping to financially support their lifestyle, including private schools, luxury vacations twice a year, and their 10,000-square-foot mansion. Marcus's parents, on the other hand, were disabled and struggled financially.

As Marcus told his money story, I learned that he grew up in a low-income neighborhood and both his parents were compulsive debtors. Marcus had many money shame cover-up behaviors, such as driving a luxury car; wearing expensive clothes; and owning a boat, motor bikes, and a mansion.

I asked him what it felt like to be a black man living in a white world.

Marcus was both stunned and relieved at the question. He said no one had ever asked him that. As we talked, it became clear that living in a white world was a huge source of his shame. He continually felt he was not measuring up—at work, at home, at his kids' school, driving his Mercedes, going to the grocery store, walking down the street with his wife, at his in-laws' house. Everywhere he went, he was swimming in toxic shame. No wonder he could not launch in his career.

Marcus lived in chronic fear and anger, and felt powerless and hopeless much of the time. He abused alcohol and sugar, causing physical illness. Although only forty, he was a type 2 diabetic.

The money detox helped Marcus name his money shame and identity the triggers. He was shocked to uncover that his source of unworthiness was attached to being black and struggling to balance that with living in a white world of privilege with his wife and children. He wept and wept, and eventually his loving wife joined us, and the truth was let out.

I watched Marcus go from hopelessness to joy. He was able to practice new behaviors that stemmed from his new sense of self-worth. After a few months, he had built up the confidence and courage to interview for his dream job as head chef of a world-class restaurant. It was not a surprise to me that he got the job.

Trading a Rolex for Prayer Beads

When you're generous in spirit, what you give comes back to you, in some form, sooner or later. By the same token, if you're not good at receiving, you won't be able to receive.

Before I went through a total crash and burn, I never allowed myself to receive from others—neither gifts nor money. If someone came for dinner and brought me a gift, chocolate, or wine, I would send them home with it. "I have enough, you take it home to your family." If I received money, I would gift it to someone else. Not only did I refuse to receive gifts, but I didn't understand the critical importance of the principle of the law of giving and receiving. I was receiving from a space of lack. I thought, "How can I accept this? If I do, I will owe them and I'll have to pay them back. They are only giving because they feel sorry for me."

I was stuck in my shame, unable to take in other people's love. I always had to be the one who hosted all the parties. I bought all the food. When I went out to dinner with friends, nobody else paid; I was always wrestling somebody for the bill. I was a delusional bigshot who thought that if I handled everything financially, then others would give me what I needed from them: love and belonging.

I didn't know how to ask for help, as my codependency made me the rescuer for everybody else. It was inconceivable for me to allow others to assist me in any way. This behavior was learned and went back to my childhood inherited money beliefs. My mom was not able to receive help easily. She never felt good enough, and she taught me how to give but not how to receive. How could she? Not receiving was in our DNA.

For nearly a year, in the aftermath of the financial crisis, I had no income. During that time, people gifted me money so I could survive as I transitioned from being a mortgage broker to being a financial planner. Friends stepped up in significant ways to assist me. Tara gifted me a car and thousands of dollars. Four dear friends in North Florida got together, decided to take action, and sent random checks each month. But I didn't see any of this money as a gift. I saw it as loans and felt obligated to pay it back. That was hugely stressful and caused me to become increasingly isolated because it was hard to face my friends. I lived in a cloud of guilt and shame. I could barely move most days. I was so frozen with fear, panic, and stress that I couldn't muster the strength to tell anyone what was happening to me emotionally. I become profoundly aware of the shame and pain Keith lived in all those years when he was dependent on others for money. It became crystal clear to me why he reached the point of taking his life.

I can say today that I wasn't doing everything I could at that point to turn things around. I was only getting by because people were giving me money. I wasn't turning to God or coming to terms with my self-worth.

During that time, in addition to financial gifts, friends dropped by my house to share a meal or to invite me to walk on the beach. This continued for two years, and it profoundly changed my life. I felt unconditional love. I had always felt very alone and isolated, and that I had to have money for people to love me. I learned a priceless gift: receiving love was the antidote for shame and isolation. Friends starting telling me the truth about how my refusal of their love felt. They told me not allowing them to do anything for me in the past had blocked them from experiencing the natural joy and love that arise in the process of giving and receiving. When I was finally able to let them in and learn how to receive, a significant shift occurred in my financial prosperity consciousness. Ironically, by developing more humility, my sense of self-worth and net worth increased. My new career soon took off, and money began rolling in.

In early 2009, when I was heading toward bankruptcy, a friend suggested I consider selling my home. My house was part of a big dream and related to my worth. I was living on the ocean, a childhood dream, and had earned my right to be there. Selling felt like the ultimate failure. It took many months to get the willingness to consider selling. I started with the math. In the finance world, you're trained to strip everything down to the facts and the numbers, leaving the emotions out. Every time I did the math on my expenses and income in relation to the house, I saw as clear as day that I was under an enormous amount of financial pressure to keep it up. So I became willing to visualize living somewhere new and possibly renting. I drove around the community and asked friends if they knew of any rental properties in the area. Still, I couldn't get past the idea that I would no longer be a homeowner. I had a lot of shame about that. Even though my logical mind was intact, my internal shame and that little girl in Alicia's driveway were driving the bus. It took four years to let go, and let me tell you, I was dragged there.

Friends also suggested I sell anything of value before I went through bankruptcy. That would provide me with additional cash on hand. So I looked around my home at all of the expensive things I owned and began the process of clearing out. One of the first things I came across was a Rolex watch. To me, that Rolex represented a diamond engagement ring. On one occasion, when I failed to make it to the altar, a friend suggested I trade the ring that had been given back to me for something else. The jewelry store where I had purchased the ring allowed me to trade it for the Rolex. I put the Rolex in a drawer because I was wearing a Cartier I'd bought for myself in my early twenties which had deep meaning and value. But the Rolex was gold, and I saw it as an investment. When I came across the Rolex during my downsizing process, the price of gold happened to be through the roof. So I decided to sell it, along with a platinum diamond ring and some other jewelry that was attached to old relationships and previous heartbreaks.

I went through every part of my home and had an online open house. Not only did the Rolex go in a bidding war, but I sold my racing bike, office chairs, Starbucks barista home espresso machine, cameras, dining room furniture, fancy kitchen knives, lots of William Sonoma dishes and cookbooks, and those 222 shoes from my shopping days at Nordstrom. It was a breakthrough.

I felt enormous relief and satisfaction that I had risen to the occasion. My belief in myself rose up. I could come back. I saw my old self, my grit, and my resilience. I had been buried in shame and grief. The house cleaning was a healing experience. I didn't know it at the time, but I had turned the corner toward becoming a minimalist as I released the evidence of my emotional clutter. I had replaced that clutter with closer, more trusting friendships and with a new wealth of spiritual practices. Meditation and prayer were the precious jewels I needed in my life. I had discovered a knowing inside me that I could rely on. As I moved on to my new career, my sense of self-worth allowed me to be of maximum service to others, not just work for money or ego strokes.

With the clutter gone, I was curious to learn about giving from my new spiritual consciousness—the "enough money" mindset. I began a new practice of giving, called tithing, or *zakat, dana, dakshina* or *tzedakah* in other world religious. *Tithing* was a dirty word in the house I grew up in. I often heard Peter say to my mother, as she left for church, "Don't give them all my money. That church is running a scam. They make you feel guilt and shame to get you to give." I had to do a lot of work to release Peter's money belief about giving.

Here's what works for me with tithing. I take one-tenth (*tithe* means one-tenth) of my gross income either daily, weekly, or monthly as I receive money and I give it to people. I give it to people who remind me of who I am and people who help my soul grow. For example, I might give to a friend who makes me laugh when I really needed it, my hairdresser for making me feel extra beautiful, or an author for waking me up again. I also give to my spiritual community.

I have made giving a spiritual practice. I buy a stack of beautiful greeting cards from my favorite local bookstore. On Sundays, I reflect on the week and send money. Each card begins with "Dear One, Thank you for reminding me of who I am. Please accept this tithe as a symbol of my appreciation and love for you."

This is the most joyful act of giving I have ever known. The tenth is returned to me almost immediately. For example, I'll get a new client or a refund or a gift of money in the mail. The point is to give whatever you can from a place of gratitude and feeling that you have enough and you are enough.

Identifying your spending priorities and determining what is of greatest importance to you in the physical world are key tasks in this element of the money detox process. But it doesn't stop there. A spiritual crisis calls for a spiritual solution. You have to dig deeper if you want to find a sense of worth that is as lasting as bedrock. If your worth is tied to a house, what happens when the house burns down? If your worth is tied to your job, what happens when you lose that job? If your worth is tied to your partner, what happens when he or she falls ill and dies? Those are all distressing circumstances, and sources of grief, but they need not undermine your ultimate sense of self-worth and your net worth

The last exercise in this chapter will help you identify your lasting source of worth.

Sofia's Story

When I first met with Sofia, she told me she had been working at her job for five years and was not making the same money as the men in her office. She said, "I'm so frustrated, I just want to quit!"

As Sofia began the money detox, I learned more about her story. She grew up in a large Catholic Cuban family, where she was the only girl, amidst nine brothers. The focus of the family was on the men. Her mother, born in Cuba, had very traditional views about a woman's place in the world.

A millennial raised in the United States, Sofia was not interested in a life at home. She was a brilliant young attorney, with high goals. However, she had a difficult time speaking up for herself, both at home and at work. The prospect of asking for more power or money was a cause of shame for her. So she watched in silence as her male colleagues received promotions and bonuses, while she worked her butt off, put in many late nights, and always went the extra mile, yet remained inadequately rewarded.

Sofia identified money beliefs she had inherited from her mother. One in particular played over and over in her head: "God intended for women to stay at home, have children, and take care of the men." Sofia knew that was not what she believed herself, but she was nonetheless playing right into that belief at work.

I asked her, "What is the fear that keeps you from speaking up to your boss and asking for a raise?"

She said, "I'm afraid I will lose my job."

I asked what evidence she had that this would happen.

She thought about that for a minute, then said, "Uh, none I guess."

"Okay," I said. "Are you ready to ask for a raise?"

Sofia and I focused on building her self-worth. We reviewed all of her life accomplishments—what I call our *true assets.* And she had many! She graduated top in her class, was class president, and won a spelling bee championship, to name just a few.

That day in my office, Sofia felt so empowered that she drafted a letter to her boss asking for a $30,000 annual pay increase to develop and implement a much-needed training program at the firm. One week later, she had a meeting with the partners, where she laid out the strategy and plan. One month later, Sofia was offered a $50,000 pay increase and a promotion to implement the new program. One year later, she was up for partner.

SELF-DIRECTION #9: Measuring Worth

1. In your money journal, make a list of whatever you consider a source of worth in your life (for example, my job, my intellect, my annuity, my paycheck, my loyalty, my inheritance, my house, my boat, my golf rank, my generosity, my music, my car, my cooking, my clothes, my jewelry).

2. Go through the list, item by item, and ask yourself, "On a scale of 1 to 5 how worthy does this make me feel?" (1 = no impact on my worth, 5 = high impact on my worth). For example: My car = 1, it gets me from place to place but it doesn't affect my true worth. My friends = 5, when I'm with my friends, they reinforce my self-worth.

3. When you've gone through your list, ask yourself, "Is there anything that isn't on this list that gives me a lasting sense of worth that can't be broken, no matter what?"

6

Make Forgiveness a Daily Practice

If there's any debt in your life and you want to get out of debt, the quickest way to do so is to forgive.

— Edwene Gaines

From an early age, I had strong ideas about where I wanted my life to go and what I wanted to happen. I began working with a therapist when I was twenty years old, and it was immediately clear that my life's vision wasn't manifesting the way I imagined. I was glad the therapist was there, because I was secretly counting on her to rescue me. Little did I expect what was coming.

After she had listened to my story, she said, "You're going to have to learn how to forgive your abusers. Yes, you were sexually abused. That happened. But the question now is what you want to do about it. Do you want to remain stuck?"

I said, "I don't want to be stuck. I want to be happy. I want to be free. I want to have a family. Maybe I want children."

"For you to do that, you'll have to forgive your parents." She explained that she could help me forgive my parents for their wrongs by understanding their past, their pain and struggle. I didn't have to forget, but I had to forgive them for making horrible choices.

I was completely thrown by that. "You've got to be kidding me! I have to forgive my abusers? I have to forgive my mother for staying with my abuser? I have to forgive my father for leaving me? I have to forgive my stepfather for molesting me? I don't think so."

I couldn't believe what I was hearing. This wasn't the rescue I'd been hoping for.

"For you to forgive them, you can't drink or drug to numb the pain. You keep crashing cars because you drink and drive, and you're reckless. If you continue to drink and do drugs, you're going to die. Do you want to die?"

I said no because I didn't want to die. But I didn't want to feel the pain, either. I didn't yet get that forgiveness was the way out of that pain. I couldn't let go, because I was too comfortable in it. It was all I knew. So I just held on and kept wallowing in it. The pain manifested in a lot of physical ways: headaches, stomach problems, and weight gain. I was immersed in pain. But I just kept walking, with that pain always there, to the next therapy session, to the next 12-step meeting, to the next retreat, to the next inpatient treatment for the next addiction.

Humility and Compassion Lead to Forgiveness

Often I hear people say, "I can't forgive!" They get to that point in their money detox, and they screech to a halt. Forgiveness feels like a step too far. They say, "I hate her; I can't forgive what she did to me." Or "I never want to see his face again. How could I ever say I'm sorry?" So many reactions are based on fear, resentment, and anger. I understand them because I've been there.

Now I see that two characteristics are essential for forgiveness: humility and compassion.

As beginners, we know that we don't yet know what it is that we are learning, so there is humility. Compassion for others starts with self-compassion. Give yourself a break. In my case, I had to be willing to examine what Amrita said to me. Rather than close off, shut down, curl up, and die, I remained willing to hear her words and ask myself if they were valid. Was I a victim? Was I crying and whining? While I had my reasons for feeling distressed, her words were indeed valid. Staying stuck in victimhood was not serving me. With her support, I opened my heart to God. I learned to be willing to be humble and to have compassion for myself.

It can get lonely if you don't start filling that God-sized hole with God. We tend to fill that hole with other stuff. Material possessions. Relationships. Money. Substances. When you start filling it with God instead, greater willingness kicks in.

When you welcome a higher power into your life, it is easier to see how that higher power also exists in every other human being on this planet. It's in there somewhere! Even in your abuser. You don't have to like or even accept what an abuser did to you to recognize that the light of God exists within that person. Recognizing that, you can start to examine what went wrong in that person's life that led to him or her being abusive. Often, people who were themselves abused are the ones who become the worst abusers. It is a vicious cycle. The first step in breaking that cycle is having compassion for yourself, and the second step is having compassion for them. That foundation gives you what you need to move into forgiveness.

"I Was Wrong"

No one could have explained to me what was going to happen once I grasped that little thing called *forgiveness*. Forgiveness, I discovered, is the path to more joy, freedom, expression, truth; it is the path out of suffering and the path to living in your authentic self. Really, it's the path to everything that matters!

Forgiveness is a spiritual practice, and science also supports it. Loren Toussaint and other researchers who've been studying forgiveness over the years report it has positive effects not only on our mental well-being but also on our physical health. When they are able to forgive, people experience less depression, anxiety, and hostility, and are less susceptible to drug dependence and substance abuse. Forgiveness also reduces cortisol levels, leading to such benefits as lower blood pressure, less risk of heart attack, and better sleep.[1]

When I started peeling back the layers of shame I'd insulated myself from for so long, I stepped into my authentic self. I realized I had been blaming the world for all my (financial) problems: "George Bush! He deregulated the banks, and Wall Street's greed started this whole mess." "Keith might be alive if his mortgage broker stopped him from refinancing his house three times in one year." In other words, "Poor me, poor me, pour me a drink."

I had to stop pointing my figure at everyone else but me. If I was to truly change, I had to start looking in the mirror. It wasn't easy, but when I started doing that, I was able to forgive myself and accept myself. And after that, I was ready to extend the hand of forgiveness. At long last, I was able to see the importance of forgiveness.

1. Loren L. Toussaint, and Everett Worthington, *Forgiveness and Health: Scientific Evidence and Theories Relating Forgiveness to Better Health*, ed. D. R. Williams (Dordrecht: Springer, 2015).

It took a long time, I must tell you. This process of investigating, identifying, and ultimately forgiving isn't fast. Many people won't choose to complete this level of work; they want a quick fix. The truth is that you have to become willing to walk a long, and at times incredibly uncomfortable, path.

You can't get to the full experience of forgiveness by yourself. You need other people to help you examine your thinking, especially during the early stages. There is too much to sort through and fix on your own. My feelings of shame and unworthiness kept me from getting any form of support for years. Instead, I used money to armor up and look like I had it all together. I could pay for a therapist. I had enough money to go to an expensive treatment center. But I was kidding myself: all those people were hired staff, and recruiting them to help me was merely my way of introducing another level of control, another way to avoid actual intimacy. Besides, often when you pay people, they just tell you what you want to hear.

As a coach, I make a point of doing the opposite. When people come to me, I say, "I'm going to tell you the truth—with love, compassion, no blame, no judgment. Blame and judgment kill the soul, and you are here to rise up. You may not be paying me for the whole truth, but it is essential for your growth to hear from a trusted friend what you can't see that blocks you from your blessings." The truth gets blocked when we are in protection and armored with shame. Self-love and self-compassion, over time, will allow you to put down the armor and thrive.

Eventually, I reached the point in my own money detox where I was ready to forgive, to make amends. As I worked with my sponsor, I realized it was time to give up blame, judgment, and shame. It was time to give up all the tools and protection schemes I'd used, including my grandiosity, elitism, and intellect. The only way I could accomplish this was to admit I was wrong and apologize. This was not going to happen without the help of my higher power and a human. I had to ask God to help me through the process, and I needed another human—my sponsor—to examine my thinking all along the way.

Making amends marked the first time I had ever said to another human being, "I was wrong." I always felt like a victim of my circumstances, so being wrong never occurred to me. But I was finally ready to get out of the pain loop of blame. The first step was to make a list of all the persons I had harmed and become willing to make amends to them all. My sponsor guided me every step of the way.

It's important to do this with another person because sometimes we think we owe someone amends, but after further examination, that may not be necessary. For example, I thought I owed a friend amends for not speaking to her for a month after she stole my credit card and went on a shopping spree. Turns out she was in the wrong.

My sponsor and God help me find the words to say when

I was making amends. I would say, "I was wrong for the way I treated you," and then give a list of all I had done. I also had to be willing to hear from the person because I might have harmed him or her in a way I was not aware of. It was not all about me. So I followed up with "Is there anything I missed or anything you'd like to say?"

My first try was with one of my many ex-girlfriends. I called her up and asked if she would meet me at a local restaurant. She agreed.

Over coffee, I proceeded to tell her all the things I had done to her that were wrong. I said, "I was wrong, and I'm sorry." I apologized for calling her a gold digger and dating me for money. I apologized for shaming her for choosing to drive a twelve-year-old-car. I apologized for the times I had talked about her substandard apartment in a shaming way, and bought her new furniture without asking if she wanted it. I apologized for buying clothes for her simply because I didn't like what she wore. I apologized for shaming her over the way I felt she manipulated me sexually to get what she wanted. I apologized for all that and more.

During the conversation, I witnessed her have a healing moment. My heart changed in that moment, as well. I felt a deep sense of humility and love. To complete making amends, I asked if there was anything I didn't mention that had harmed her.

She replied yes. She said she had wanted to hear these words from me for years, but there was more. She proceeded to tell me how my judgments and criticism of her had affected her self-esteem and how she never felt I accepted her for who she was.

We had a big cry and hugged goodbye. But when I got in my car and drove off, I had an old thought: *Wow! That didn't go the way I thought it would!* I was pissed because she hadn't said, "Wow, you've changed so much. I love you. Let's get back together." I still wanted her to pursue and adore me. I had been sure that once I came clean, she'd want me back.

On the way home, I called my sponsor and told her I felt wonderful during the amends, but now I felt angry. I didn't feel any better. I certainly didn't feel the way I hoped to feel. Nor did I feel I had forgiven myself completely. I was shocked at my anger and felt sorry for myself. All she said was "Yeah, it sucks when someone doesn't want to get back together with you, doesn't it?" We need truth tellers in our lives!

Making amends to all my various exes was a pure act of will and courage. It was the first time I'd ever felt truly sorry for what I had done. I looked at each one, face to face, and watched the tears fall as I confessed things I had never been willing or able to own before. When we were together, I was riddled with shame, and as a protection, I made them wrong all the time. Now I could see their souls in ways I had never been able to. I realized all I had missed. The money detox was working: my self-worth and net worth were increasing.

SELF-DIRECTION #10: I Forgive Myself

The ticket to financial freedom is forgiveness. Forgiveness begins with yourself. Edwene Gaines introduced me to this powerful forgiveness exercise.[2]

Before we can truly forgive, we must make space in our heart by releasing our blame.

1. Start by writing in your journal:

- I am over with feeling shame about ____ [fill in the blank]

- I am over with feeling sorry for myself about ____

- I am no longer going to blame __ for ____

2. Next write in your journal: I forgive myself totally and completely for____ [fill in the blank].

Examples:

- I forgive myself totally and completely for criticizing my spouse or partner for losing their job.

- I forgive myself totally and completely for gossiping about my neighbor and their home going into foreclosure.

---

2. Edwene Gaines, *The Four Spiritual Laws of Prosperity: A Simple Guide to Unlimited Abundance* (Harlan, IA: Rodale Books, 2005).

- I forgive myself totally and completely for stealing that candy bar in fifth grade.

- I forgive my mother totally and completely for marrying for money not love.

- I forgive my father totally and completely for not financially supporting my mother and leaving her to raise three children on her own.

- I forgive my grandmother totally and completely for refusing to pay the electric bill when my mother's paycheck was delayed.

3. Write out your statement 35 times in the morning and 35 times in the evening for seven consecutive days. Write the same thing, line after line.

If writing is not for you, stand in front of a mirror, look into your eyes, and repeat the statement as many times as you desire for seven days.

If you miss a day, start over.

4. After you have worked on one statement for a week (or longer), select another and begin the process again. Or take a break. Forgiveness is a a lifetime practice. You will have many opportunities to come back to this exercise. What I want to you know is that it works, it really really does. I have seen it open the flood gates of blessings in many people's lives.

Ruth's Story

Ruth told me her money story. First she talked about her mother. Her mother grew up in a blue-collar family, with four siblings. Every summer, her mother went to live with an extremely wealthy aunt and uncle, who had no children of their own. She loved being part of their lavish lifestyle.

Ruth said her mother grew up and married a wealthy businessman. She threw parties and began drinking heavily.

As a child, Ruth watched her mother become a con. She stole money from Ruth's father and spent thousands on clothes. Eventually Ruth's father divorced her mother. Ruth said, "My mother received very little money from the divorce. She went deeper and deeper into drugs and alcohol. A few years later, penniless, she overdosed on Valium."

Ruth said, "I am in the same situation now with my husband. I don't want to become penniless or die." She said she was hundreds of thousands of dollars in debt. She had spent all of her $400,000 annual salary on clothes, jewelry , trips, and collectibles. She was one step away from divorce and was taking up to a dozen Valiums a day.

Ruth agreed to go through the money detox and get help for her prescription drug abuse. When she got to the element of forgiveness, it was not easy for Ruth to forgive herself. She had so much shame about her money behaviors and felt deep guilt for not forgiving her mother before her death.

She owned the statement *I forgive myself totally and completely for not being there for Mom.*

It took several months to work through the pain, but Ruth was willing. She kept at it. A turning point came when her husband began to join our sessions. They had many hard conversations about their money behaviors, beliefs, resentments, and patterns. The love they had for each other carried them through, and within a few months, they had a plan and a set of new tools that allowed them to feel safe to stay in the marriage. They forgave themselves and each other totally and completely. Today they are debt free and planning for their retirement.

Breaking the Cord of Shame

Naturally, two of the people at the top of my forgiveness list were my mother and Peter. They were my biggest abusers. Their abuse was spiritual, physical, emotional, and psychological.

On Easter weekend, I invited them to my house in Florida. It was the first time I had asked Peter to my home. I went to play golf with him, and afterward, we went for lunch at a coffee shop. I told him that I had not forgiven him for the abuse, and that I needed to do that. I acknowledged that as a result of not my forgiving him, I had continually tried to get others to see what he did and how bad he was. In this way, I had continued to cause him harm for years. I had interfered with his marriage to my mom. I had interfered with his relationship with his son and my older brothers.

I'll never forget the look on his face as I was speaking. He was absolutely shocked.

Although Peter hadn't owned up to his actions when I confronted him during my first rehab stay at age twenty-two, he had done so some years later. About a year after I moved to Florida, Peter's son Thomas dropped out of school because of drugs, was convicted of a felony, and went to jail. Peter called me because he was so distraught that his son had committed a crime. On that call, he acknowledged his actions for the first time and apologized for what he had done to me. I was twenty-nine at the time, and I said I forgave him. But I didn't. Not really.

On the day I made amends in the coffee shop, Peter started to cry. He said, "I'm so sorry. I was in such a bad place in my life back then. I don't know why I did that to you."

I said, "I'm sorry, too."

He didn't want to accept my apology and projected it off himself very quickly. "How can you forgive me? How can you say to me what you're saying to me?"

In the years leading up to this moment, I had asked my

mother about Peter's childhood. Peter had endured emotional and physical abuse.

I thought, *We all have a story. How can I not forgive him?* I didn't say I would forget what happened. But I became willing to understand his pain. It was a healing moment for us.

I also had to forgive my mother. Believe it or not, that was much more difficult than forgiving Peter.

I started by examining her role in my life. My mother had kept me silent for years by saying, "Don't tell anyone you're gay. Don't tell anyone my husband abused you. Don't tell anyone you're a drug addict. Don't tell anyone you're an alcoholic. Don't tell anybody our secrets." Her whole line of defense was "don't put shame on me."

I recalled all the ways she had prevented me from putting shame on the family. She did it in subtle ways. She was never mean. Her primary tactic was to play the poor-me victim, which was designed to make me feel that whenever I did anything "wrong," I was harming her more than she'd already been harmed by life's cruelties. In a twisted way, she encouraged me to believe that if I were to be powerful in the world, then I was going to hurt her.

I subconsciously obeyed that message for many years. It was nothing short of extraordinary, cunning, and baffling how my mother manipulated me by being a victim. If I were to win, then conversely that meant she had to fail. Her manipulation prevented me from having a loving relationship with another human being. I've seen similar dynamics in almost every one of my clients: the dysfunction always goes back to the mother or the father. But it's usually the mother, as she has such power over us.

During her visit to Florida, I sat with my mother on a park bench one day. She had recently been diagnosed with breast cancer. I asked why she had stayed in her marriage so long, when it was detrimental to her mind, body, and spirit.

Her response was simple: "Where would I go? I don't have enough money to make it on my own. I don't want to be a burden to my children."

My mother's pain was evident in her response. I could see the childlike fear that kept her feeling unworthy of love. My heart broke for her. I realized at this point how enmeshed our relationship had become and how I had let my happiness be dependent on hers.

To break the cord, I had to become entirely responsible for my own happiness. That was no small thing. Only if I didn't let her pull my strings would I be free to shine.

The impact my mother's low self-esteem had on my life was profound. Understanding her pain allowed me to feel compassion for her and to forgive her. It made it possible to see the harm I caused her over the years by not accepting her.

When I became willing to make amends to her, I was able to say, "Mom, I was wrong for making you wrong when you didn't go to therapy after Keith's death. I was wrong for being angry at you for not going to Al-Anon to help yourself and your four alcoholic children. I was wrong for judging and punishing you for staying in your marriage." Making amends opened my heart in a way I could not have imagined. My heart had been shut down because I hadn't forgiven, and I didn't even realize to what degree.

This has become one of my greatest gifts as a human. As a money coach, I am off my perch; I'm in the trenches. I can truly and honestly empathize with people's pain. I can empathize with living in a family shattered by shame and abuse. I can relate to the impact that has on finances. I had to have a paradigm shift in my thinking before I could get to forgiveness. And I forgave myself, as well. I tell people to forgive themselves first. But I didn't know that when I was going through the money detox; I forgave myself last.

Much of the personal growth work I do today is about self-compassion and self-forgiveness. I focus every day on continually forgiving myself. If somebody does something that reminds me of my past and myself, then I quickly forgive that person and myself. I have come along way from the Starbucks meeting with Keith and Karen. Understanding a person's past and how it creates that person's present is a very kind and loving act. I see it now as the door way to transformation.

Andrew's Story

When I met Andrew, he said, "My wife left me for another man after twenty-five years of marriage. She depleted all our savings and ran up thousands of dollars in debt on my credit cards. I am so furious, I can't function, and my job is at risk."

Andrew's money story was riveting. When Andrew was eighteen, his mother and father went missing. Several years went by before the police solved the case. His mother's and father's remains were found in an old abandoned cabin in the mountains by hikers. There was a note. Andrew's mother wrote, "Your father and I spent the last few years traveling the world. We ate, we drank, we shopped, we lived like royals. We died happy."

Andrew was informed by the police that they had found dozens of fake IDs and credit cards along with the note. It was all planned out. They never intended to live beyond their indulgences.

Andrew had blocked this memory from his consciousness for decades, only to wake up in a familiar feeling of betrayal, anger, and depression at the age of sixty-two. He was accustomed to using denial as a way to protect himself from the loss of his mother and father, and unknowingly had attracted a wife with a money mindset similar to that of his family.

He was full of resentment and anger that nearly cost him

his life. He was very close to suicide on many days. Something inside of him knew that it was his job to break this legacy for his daughter and grandchildren. We dove deep into his parent's childhood to understand their money story and what may have led to their choices. Andrew stayed with the process with a lot of love and support. I will never forget the look of peace on his face when I heard him say, "I forgive my mother, I forgive my father, I really, really do."

SELF-DIRECTION #11: Practice Loving-Kindness

Once you have begun to self-forgive and are feeling more acceptance of yourself, it is time to contemplate making amends with important people in your life. Remember, this is not about condoning what they did (saying their behavior was acceptable) or forgetting the pain you felt. It's about forgiveness for them as human beings, flaws and all.

You can practice loving-kindness by allowing those you want to make amends to come before you in your meditation and offering your love unconditionally to them. It may not be in your best interest to make an amends directly to a person, but when you do it within your heart, have faith that, on some level, the person can receive it.

Loving-kindness practice:[3]

Please visualize someone or those who you love sitting in front of you. Open your heart and say to them:

> May you be safe from inner and outer harm.
> May you be free from guilt, shame, and hatred.
> May you enjoy physical and mental well-being.
> May you live with the ease of an open heart.
> May you go beyond your inner darkness and awaken
> to your radiant true nature as boundless love.

3. Reprinted by permission from Dharmata Foundation, dharmata.org

Now, please visualize someone or those you find to be challenging or difficult sitting in front of you. Open your heart and say to them:

> May you be safe from inner and outer harm.
> May you be free from guilt, shame, and hatred.
> May you enjoy physical and mental well-being.
> May you live with the ease of an open heart.
> May you go beyond your inner darkness and awaken
> to your radiant true nature as boundless love.

Now, imagine everyone in the world is sitting in front of you. Open your heart and say to them:

> May you be safe from inner and outer harm.
> May you be free from guilt, shame, and hatred.
> May you enjoy physical and mental well-being.
> May you live with the ease of an open heart.
> May you go beyond your inner darkness and awaken
> to your radiant true nature as boundless love.

May we express loving kindness toward each other so that war, conflict and every form of strife come to an end, allowing peace and harmony to pervade the entire world.

Forgiving My Father

A few months after Keith's death in 2007, I reconnected with my biological father for the first time since I was a small child. I reached out to him at that time because he and Keith had developed a relationship over the years, and I knew that my father must be in a lot of pain following the loss of his youngest son. I had also learned that he sent money to my sister-in-law and the kids following Keith's death.

I handwrote a letter to my father and included some photographs of my brother and me, along with pics of his grandchildren. That letter wasn't easy to write, but it opened the door for connection.

A few weeks later, my father called and we spoke for three hours.

During the call, my father explained his side of the story. He told me what had happened to him and why he left our family. He was open, honest, and apologetic, and it was a very healing moment for me.

After that, he proceeded to jump in and act like a dad. He sent birthday cards and flowers and called numerous times over the next year.

But the truth was that even though I had made the initial contact, I was not ready for a relationship. I was overwhelmed by grief over my circumstances. His efforts to communicate were too much for me to handle. So I didn't reciprocate.

Our first in-person meeting took place seven years later, in June 2014. Every year since Keith's death, I had been participating in the American Foundation of Suicide Prevention's overnight walk. This seventeen-mile walk takes place from dusk to dawn to raise money and awareness about the prevention of suicide. Each year, it is held in a different city. In 2014, it was in Boston, near my hometown. My father lives in the area, so I reached out to him and asked for a visit.

He agreed to meet.

I felt ready to meet him. I had done a lot of work around understanding my father's childhood. Understanding that he could not have done better, I went to the visit with an open heart and offered him my compassion and forgiveness, knowing that forgiveness has the power to heal.

When I arrived, my father was outside, pacing his yard. He was tall and thin, with long hair pulled back in a ponytail. I would've known him anywhere because my oldest brother James looks identical.

As I stepped out of the car, I gave him a huge smile. I could see the love in his eyes for me, and it touched me deep in my soul. I knew then that a father's love for his children never dies, and I felt the same way about him.

We spent the next six hours sitting in his garden, having

lunch and sharing stories. I could've stayed all day and into the next day, as it was such a wonderful, healing visit.

If you have grown up not knowing one of your parents, I can tell you there's a part of you in that parent that you don't see anywhere else. For example, my mother and I physically look very much alike, but our personalities are very different. I always felt a strange sense of wondering about why I was the way that I was. I learned where I came from that day when I sat with my father, as he and I have similar intellect and personality traits. We like a lot of the same things, including flowers, gardening, cooking, taking things apart, and fixing things. I saw that the part of me that likes to dig deep and get to the root of the problem came from my dad. I remember my mother saying as I was growing up, "You're just like your father." It always seemed to be during times when she was unhappy with me, however, so I internalized her observances as meant to make me wrong or bad.

My father confirmed that he gave his children up for financial reasons. He confirmed all the stories my mother had told us. That day, I discovered that my father would have been a really good dad. He had some healthy core beliefs and strong internal boundaries. Sadly, once again, money and shame robbed my father, mother, brothers, and me of a life together.

Marlene's Story

When she explored her money story, Marlene focused on her father. She said he treated her differently than he treated her sister. She said, "He loved my sister more; she was smarter, more like him. I was more like my mother, whom he eventually divorced."

Marlene's resentments centered around her father's lack of generosity toward her with money. He was wealthy, she said, but would not give her a dime. When she bought her first car, her father loaned her $2000.

Then Marlene lost her job and missed her monthly car payment.

Her father phoned and told her that her grandmother, who had recently died, had left her $5000. Marlene desperately needed the money since she had not found another job. However, her father made her wait six months for the money. When she finally received it, she discovered he had deducted the $2000 she had borrowed for the car, plus interest.

This created a huge resentment for Marlene that manifested in a tit-for-tat, fairness money mindset in all her relationships. She found it impossible to be generous with her money. She became resentful of her husband and any friends when she felt they didn't play fair with money. She said, "I became secretive and dishonest with money and often manipulated my husband to get what I wanted."

A few decades after the car loan incident, Marlene's mother died suddenly. Marlene had not forgiven her mother for her part in Marlene's childhood money story. This led to some very painful years for Marlene, as she struggled to do the work around forgiving her mother.

Marlene told me she was not willing to go through all that again. Her father was now ninety-seven, and she wanted to do the work now, before it was too late. She started with self-compassion, and with forgiving herself for her resentment and stinginess in her relationship with her husband. After they had healed together, she said she was ready to approach her father.

In Marlene's case, there was not much direct talk about money. Her father was in a nursing home and had some degree of dementia. So talking about $5000 or $2000 wouldn't have been meaningful. But that didn't matter. Marlene started going to visit him regularly. She went with an attitude she described as "being in my heart" and she focused on appreciating her father. It worked. He showered her with love and looked forward to every visit. Marlene felt profoundly changed by the forgiveness process. She told me, "My father and I are having a love affair these days."

Marie's Story

As I was writing this chapter, I asked Keith's daughter, Marie, my niece, if she would be willing to offer her perspective. She readily agreed. The following paragraphs are her own words, taken from the letter she wrote me.

Growing up, I was always told to save the money I was given or that I earned through chores. But then I saw my family freely spending money and arguing about it afterward. I developed the idea that money must not be a good thing, but we all need it and want it. Money caused many problems for my family, as I've always felt like we don't have enough. I believe I've gotten this idea from many observations. I never knew much about saving, as I was always given what I wanted somehow. I was taught that I earned these rewards (or these things) because I did well in school or was a good daughter, so it was okay to spend money on me. I was taught that if you are deserving of it, you can have it, no matter the situation. At twenty years old, I understand that sometimes you have to make sacrifices. Now when I have the extra money to treat myself I will, but only once all of my bills are paid, as that is my priority.

I feel that my father feared money because he knew we did not have enough for the lifestyle we were living. We had a large home for four people, filled with food, toys, games, and the luxuries of going on family vacations on top of this. He coped with his stress through his expensive habits of drinking and smoking cigarettes. When he passed, my family's money situation naturally became much worse. My mother was too mentally unstable to work for six months to almost a year after he died. Our home was foreclosed upon, and we were forced to leave and rent out a small townhome from an old family friend until that rent became too much for us to afford as well.

My brother left for college, and I'll never understand how he managed on his own out there, mentally and financially, after everything that had happened. My mom and I moved into another family friend's one-bedroom basement. Our phone service would always get cut off due to late payments, and there were lots of problems with having a landlord. I continued at my private Catholic school, and although the tuition had risen, with the help of the school, my mom made it work. At times we faced trouble with payments, and I would feel embarrassed and ashamed if I could not participate in certain things. But my mom always tried her best, working long hours when possible. When it came to deciding on a high school, I chose a local public school to save the cost of another tuition and hopefully give my family time to save up for college for me. With the help of my grandmother, we got a nice townhome near the high school. Then my mom hurt her neck and back and was out of work for about six to eight months, making things financially tough for us.

She received some money from her job at the time, but with our lifestyle, we still experienced the cable, water, and electricity getting cut off here and there. Money is very hard for my mother and me even today.

My father's passing has affected me immensely, in both positive and negative aspects. I feel that if he had survived or simply had continued to live without suicide playing a part, I would be different. I am a very humble, well-rounded, and understanding person. I am who I am today because of him and because of the hardship that has become my own. I fear money and worship it all in the same breath.

I feel that money controls your future in most cases, which is why I worship it because I'd love for more and more to come into my blessings. But I fear money because it can change everything in a matter of seconds. I feel that money has too much power. I still struggle with money today as I've tried to take control of my life and my money in various ways, doing the best that I can with the guidance I receive from my Aunt Tammy and my therapist. I am blessed with what my life has become, but I also long for a much better future and experience with money in the years to come.

I view money as a need and a motivator. At times, as I've said, I fear not having enough of it, but I try to understand it more than be worried about it. I work two waitressing jobs currently while attending community college part-time, to earn my money today. I feel stressed most of the time about money, to be honest. But I am money conscious and feel that my journey with money can only go "up" from here, in a positive manner. I am becoming a driven and dedicated person with time, practice, and patience. I am grateful for the guidance, support, and enlightenment I receive from my Aunt Tammy, as I know this journey will be successful with her by my side every step of the way.

Today, I accept my father's actions. I understand, and I forgive him. I lack anger towards him and his actions. I dwell at times on what could have been, but I try to remind myself how blessed I am and how far I have come. I've come to understand my blessings. I am strong and peaceful. I am blessed, and I am loved.

Marie.

7

Live from a Circle of Money Blessings

If you want money more than anything, you'll be bought and sold your whole life.

— Rumi

Years ago, I used to see a Catholic priest in 12-step meetings who would say, "Get off the cross. We need the wood!" At the time, I thought I was so adept at hiding my suffering that it amused me to hear him say that. But over time, as I worked through my own money detox, those words sank in. Now I repeat them often. Because I know it is possible to go from suffering a hundred percent of the time, stuck on the cross of my own misery, to where I am today. And if I can do it, then anyone can.

With this chapter, you have reached the last element of

the money detox process, living from a circle of money blessings. Congratulations!

Before we get into what this last element entails, let's recap. The elements you have worked on so far are as follows:

Element 1: Own your money story

Element 2: Recognize your spiritual crisis

Element 3: Uncover your shame

Element 4: Identify your money beliefs

Element 5: Discover your worth

Element 6: Make forgiveness a daily practice

Element 7: Live from a circle of money blessings

Own your money story and free yourself to write a new ending. Your detox began with your willingness to dig into and tell your own story. Owning your story about money is the basis of turning your life around. By now, you should have gotten in touch with a variety of stories—real, imagined, made up, brainwashed, inherited. Write the stories down as they come to you, without censoring them or feeling shame about them, and then figure out later what they mean and how true or untrue they are.

A big part of owning your story is telling it to at least one other person. You can record your story in your money journal—and I encourage you to do that, and to keep doing that—but a journal can only provide passive support. When you tell your story to one other human being, you open yourself up to receiving active support. So make sure you can trust the person you are opening up to!

However much of your money story has been revealed thus far, know that there is more to come. It can take years to fully uncover one's money story. Allow yourself to dig deeper so more details can emerge.

Recognize your spiritual crisis and find true belonging in a higher power. Although I have called this the second element of the money detox, in truth, it is a meta-element that spans the full money detox process. Initially, you recognize that what you are going through is not a money crisis but a spiritual crisis. The real issue is deeper than your finances. That means the solution must also be deeper than just the financial level.

Ultimately, I don't believe any solution will work if it doesn't include acknowledgment of a higher power. Thinking we can fix everything that isn't working through our own power alone—the same power that has been screwing up our life for so long—is presumptuous, to say the least. In my experience, the only way out is to have some humility and put my life in God's hands.

Uncover your shame and reclaim your power. As you began to tell your money story, you also began to do self-inquiry around it. Specifically, you focused on shame and on uncovering how toxic money shame has colored and controlled your experience. Typically, shame first occurred early in your life—for example, when someone shamed you or your family for living on the wrong side of the tracks or for having every latest gadget or for being inadequate in some way related to money. That shame became toxic when it went underground in your psyche because it was just too painful to deal with.

Identify your money beliefs and their impact on your life. You then looked more closely at your toxic money shame, and identified the inherited money beliefs that caused that shame and that have kept it alive. Beliefs, such as "Money is the root of all evil," that you learned at home at an early age drove how, as you grew up, you handled money, thought about money, talked about money. For many people, inherited money beliefs take the form of a scarcity mindset, whereby they become convinced they will never have enough.

Your inherited money beliefs, combined with festering toxic shame, may have led you to develop addictions and other self-destructive habits in an attempt to fill the hole you felt in your soul with money, food, shopping, sex, drugs, love, or alcohol. The less effective those efforts, the more you may have redoubled them. Anything to avoid confronting the pain of toxic shame head on.

Discover your worth and live according to your values. When you had gone far enough into your money story and knew both the source of your shame and how your inherited money beliefs continue to shape your relationship with money, you were ready to heal. This is the element in which spiritual solutions can begin to take shape. The first spiritual solution involved discovering your worth; that is, your true worth, aside from the worth you attach to money.

In this element, you examined your values and thought about what is really important to you in life. Lifting the veil of shame hopefully allowed you to begin to make some different and healthier choices. You challenged yourself to make your spending more closely reflect your true values.

Make forgiveness a daily practice and let go of resentments so you can live freely, joyful, and creatively. In this element, you began to make amends. This began with accepting and forgiving yourself. You may have done some stuff in your life that you wish you hadn't done, but it's time to stop shaming yourself over those things and let them go. Then you went on to make amends with others in your life, including family members from whom you inherited unhealthy money beliefs and toxic shame. Forgiveness is not a one-time event, so hopefully you have incorporated it into your daily routine.

Live from a circle of money blessings and rewrite your story. Which bring us to this, the seventh and final element. In this chapter, we discuss how you can go about rewriting the ending of your story. Now that you have done some work on your money beliefs and clarified your values, you can create a positive relationship with money—one that isn't based on a scarcity mindset, but that's based on the principles of prosperity. You can learn how to set intentions and goals to make sure that you are actually doing all of those worthy things and reaping the benefits. You are also in a position now to offer service and give back to the world. In addition to reworking your relationship with money, you can rework your relationships with people.

Circles and Elements

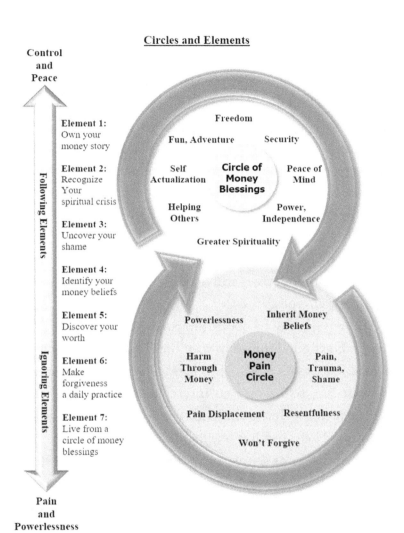

Circle of Blessings

Becoming free of money problems doesn't mean that once you have eliminated your conflicts and stresses around money, you still have to go on living with limited financial resources. The outcome of the money detox does not mean going from spending excesses to constrained frugality. It's not about extremes. When you are living from a circle of blessings, you have the freedom to actually strive for and enjoy a state of prosperity that reflects your highest aspirations. It's like the difference between merely being declared disease free and experiencing an exhilarating sense of well-being.

You are worthy of good things. You are deserving. You can embody good things in your life. There are many books available that describe techniques for achieving abundance in your life, so I won't go into that in great depth here. Suffice it to say that abundance begins with a positive state of mind. The mind has a remarkable ability to mirror our reality. It can be as simple as waking up "on the right side of the bed" and then watching as one thing after the next goes right throughout the rest of the day.

To break out of poverty and scarcity consciousness, you have to reprogram your thinking, so your conscious and subconscious minds are entirely onboard. Tell yourself you are worthy. Show yourself some love! How do you do that?

Start by ceasing all criticism of yourself (and it goes without saying, of others). The process of self-inquiry you have engaged in as part of the money detox is not criticism; it is constructive self-examination. Big difference! Accept yourself as you are. Praise yourself as much as you can. Criticism breaks down the inner spirit; praise builds it up.

I'm not saying that your thoughts control the outcome of every event in your life; obviously that is neither realistic nor even necessarily desirable. But your thoughts and feelings do have power, probably more so than you realize. If you can see it, you can be it! Your dreams can come true.

I believe the first step in actualizing your grandest vision of yourself is having the courage to share your dream with someone. That person can be a trusted friend, a coach, or a higher power. The important step is to share your vision so you can get it out there, into the realm of the possible. Then you can work on the practical steps to make it a reality. Along the way, be sure to maintain your willingness to keep moving when things don't go as planned, and remember that your dreams may shift and evolve as they come to fruition.

Joel's Story

Joel owns and runs a wellness center. He came to me because he felt grateful for the success of his business but was dissatisfied in other ways. He wanted more adventure in his life. He had a vision for his work and wanted help manifesting it. Joel loved to travel and could see himself organizing groups of people and taking them on wellness retreats around the world. He told me, "I want people to see the world and experience alternative forms of healing, and I want to make it affordable and fun!"

We discussed how he could do that, and within weeks, he had put together a small group of men and women and planned his first trip. The first stop was India. He was blown away at how quickly all the details and people fell into place.

Four years later, Joel brings groups three times a year to three destinations around the world. He gets to travel for free and enjoys meeting so many new people. He also continues to run his successful wellness center.

Intentions and Goals

I began working with a nonprofit organization following a public financial scandal. The executive director was accused of fraud and money laundering, tarnishing the reputation of the twenty-five-year-old organization. My first meeting was with the treasurer. I quickly learned that the staff were not being paid on time. My second meeting was with the board of directors.

"Where do you want to go from here?" I asked.

"We want to restore the trust of our members and repair our reputation in the community."

Perfect! They set the intention in that moment.

I worked with the board of directors to establish a strategy for their intention. Then we took swift action over the next twelve months. Here's what that looked like:

1. With the money remaining, they paid the staff all money owed in arrears.
2. They contacted the IRS, credit card companies, and state and set up payment plans.
3. They hired an interim executive director part time to organize fundraising events.
4. At every board meeting, they stated the intention and vision.

Within two years, the organization was recognized as the national association of the year (a first in their history) and had a large cash reserve (another first). Now they continue to grow and prosper.

Prosperity doesn't materialize out of the blue. God's grace is powerful, and sometimes miracles happen, but you can't count on them. That's like making God work overtime! The balance to grace is self-effort. An important aspect of prosperity is making sure you aren't just fantasizing but are working toward the things you want. The best way to do that is to set intentions and goals.

An intention declares your underlying purpose. It's what you want to see happen. Your intention can be quite broad

("I want to live in integrity with money") or it can be narrower ("I want a job that puts my creativity to use").

I like to think of goals as dreams with a deadlines. Goals are how you get your intentions to materialize. They are the concrete achievements you want to accomplish like signposts along the way. When you set goals, get very specific about the details. For example, if your intention is to get a job that involves your creativity, your goals might include (1) to get relevant training, (2) to research alternative types of jobs, (3) to interview some artists, (4) to take a job and evaluate after a period of time whether it really uses your creativity, and so on.

This aspect of living on your purpose is all about taking action. What that looks like will be different for everyone, depending on the goals they have set. Be clear with yourself: What do you want? Is it a new career? A change in location? A better relationship with people, co-workers, money, health? Perhaps you want to pay off debt, start a savings account, save for retirement, create a trust fund for someone special, donate to charity, exercise regularly, lose weight, give to your church. The possibilities are endless.

Every year I buy a new journal for all the year's intentions. On New Year's Day, I begin with a practice. I chant, meditate, and sit and write. I ask God for my word for the year. My word gives me a clean slate and provides a framework for my goal setting. In 2016, my word was *freedom*, meaning "to be liberated." I was ready to make my list of goals with the help of my higher power. The first thing that came through to me was "You will be moving, alone." This came as a surprise since I was in a relationship, and we lived together. The relationship was strained and we had been struggling for some time, but I was not ready to leave. The universe had another plan: just a few weeks later, the relationship came to a mutual ending. What followed was not the happiest year of my life, but it did free me. The deep loneliness that had been hanging on from my childhood was healed. I stayed close to God and practiced a lot of self-compassion. I truly felt liberated from my past and could see clearly that it was the best choice for both of us. When we trust and rely on God, we don't need to know how things will unfold.

If you want to speed up your goals, give them to your higher power, and hold on. The result can be powerful and a surprise.

SELF-DIRECTION #12: Affirmations

Affirmations are one valuable way to get blessings flowing in your life. You can create affirmations about your own self-worth, as well as affirmations about specific intentions you hold.

For this exercise, look into a mirror and simply say to yourself, "I love you, I really love you."

It may be difficult at first, but keep practicing, and soon you will mean and feel what you say. When you sincerely feel self-love, you open to the door to a life of wealth.

Jolene's Story

Jolene and I had been working together for a few months when she called me, terrified, from her bedroom closet. "The IRS found me. They're at my front door. I haven't paid taxes in fifteen years. I will owe them for the rest of my life."

I said, "Keep breathing. You've got this. You have been preparing for this moment. It's time to face your fear and clean up the past."

The next day, Jolene phoned the local IRS and scheduled an appointment.

I accompanied her to the meeting. She was sick, dry heaving all the way there. It was a daunting meeting, and it took many months to determine exactly how much she owed. In the end, it was even more than she had feared: $500,000.

I worked with Jolene to come up with a plan that would allow her to pay off her debt. We started with a broad question about intention: "What is your ultimate goal?"

Jolene clarified that her intention was to live in honesty and integrity with her money and to have faith that money would continue to flow in her life. We then took that intention and set step-by-step goals so Jolene could work toward it without feeling overwhelmed.

In our earlier work together, Jolene had begun her money

detox and identified the entitlement belief "You owe me." Driven by that belief, she had hopped from one multi-level marketing scam to other, leaving her parents to bail her out when things got dire. When the IRS found her, the first step in cleaning up her dishonest thinking so she could pay the debt became clear: get a steady job. Fortunately, she was able to land a good job in an industry she knew well. She also worked with the IRS and was put on a payment plan.

Jolene stayed the course, with the mindset of living in integrity and the goal of financial freedom. She made all her payments on time. As she earned more, she was able to pay the IRS more. After a few years of on-time payments, the IRS reduced her debt to $100,000.

It took Jolene four years to pay off the IRS. Over those years, she received countless bonuses, company trips, and outstanding service awards. She continues to earn more money each year. Now she is debt free, with one year of savings in the bank. She also has a group of friends who love and support her, which is a first for her.

SELF-DIRECTION #13: Smart Goals

It's a bit hard to make goal setting sound sexy. But here is an acronym that has been used for decades to help people set goals, both in professional and personal settings. Pick a goal you want to set, and then make sure it is SMART, and add the secret sauce.

Specific. Don't be too vague. It is much easier to meet a goal when you define it specifically. For example, "I will pay off all of my credit card debt in two years."

Measurable. You need to be able to measure your progress. For example, how much of your debt's principal will you pay off the first year, and how much will be interest?

Attainable. A pie-in-the-sky goal will just discourage you. Don't bite off more than you can chew. For example, to never incur another debt in your life might not be an attainable goal.

Relevant. The goal should be relevant to your greater purpose. For example, if you pay off your credit card debt, you will be able to move your family into a larger home.

Timely. Goals should have a realistic timeframe. For example, can you pay off that debt in two years or do you need three?

Here is my secret sauce:

1. In a journal dedicated to your goals, write down all your dreams, big and small.

2. Choose up to eight goals you feel passion and positive energy about. Write them in order of highest importance to you. Write out all the details. As they say, God is in the details! And write them in the present tense, as if they have already materialized.

   For example: "I am living in my new home, with a yellow door and a wraparound porch, in my favorite neighborhood." Or "I am eating healthy food, and my size 8 black pants feel like pj's."

3. Pick a date when you want to realize each goal and place the date alongside that goal.

4. Each morning and evening, upon awaking and before going to sleep, ask or pray to your higher power, "What must I change in myself to achieve my goals?" Read your goals and image achieving each goal by the date.

5. Keep your goals between you and your higher power. This adds a dimension of belonging and faith when your goals are realized. It can be a spiritual experience, and I want you to feel it. You deserve it. So mum is the word.

6. Your goals may shift: some may become clearer and

others may become uninteresting. The key is to trust yourself. You can remove goals or add new ones; however the spirit moves you is the way forward. Make your own rules with your higher power.

Give Back and Offer Service

Just as good things will come to you, you also need to give back good things to the world. A big part of this is being of service to others. That means starting to think about others' needs and problems, not just being preoccupied with your own problems. In our culture, we don't necessarily grow up thinking about serving others. But it can be a beautiful spiritual practice.

Sometimes we can be of service in unexpected ways. After I filed for bankruptcy, I felt extraordinarily free and ready for a comeback year. I began working as a financial planner with the intention of being of maximum service to others, not just working for money. With this new service mindset, I was no longer focused on being the top agent. At the end of 2009, my managing partner brought to my attention that I was one life insurance policy sale away from being the new Agent of the Year. She urged me to get that sale. I asked whom I was up against. I learned that a fellow agent who had been busting his ass all year selling insurance was the person. He really wanted to be Agent of the Year, and I didn't want to take that from him. So I quietly did not pursue that last sale. To my surprise, at our annual awards banquet, I instead received the prestigious service award. I was blown away by the power of intention.

So I encourage you do adopt a service mindset and to

start looking for ways to give back to the world. If you don't know yet what your life purpose is, start small. Serve others right within your own home or family or immediate neighborhood. Maybe picking up your elderly neighbor's mail and bringing it to her door is your way to serve right now.

If you want, you can go bigger within your workplace or community. Many people take the same skills that earn them money and put those skills into service through volunteer work. This amplifies their sense of living on your purpose. For example, a chef who works at a restaurant might offer meals at a homeless center on weekends. A doctor might take time off to travel to aid victims of a natural disaster who require medical attention. A counselor might do volunteer shifts for a crisis hotline.

As a child, I dreamed of being a therapist or a psychologist, yet the reason I didn't take those paths was because of the money. I would have had to go back to school and find a way to pay for postgraduate studies. I kept my vision alive knowing that one day I would find a way to help people. In the meantime, I expressed my desire to help with various types of service work. I knew I was on the right path when the experience of assisting someone move through something challenging rewarded me on many different levels. I started a weekly women's group for codependents as I became more disciplined in my spiritual practice. I also enjoyed mentoring women. I invited them to come to my house, and I helped them at no charge. At present, I facilitate a monthly money circle for women to discuss whatever they like around money.

In 2010, as I was carrying out my brother's legacy, I was reminded that he had always wanted to be a cop. A colleague and I approached the local sheriff's department and offered to give free financial literacy training to all the police officers, along with a follow-up meeting with their spouse or partner. This went over so well that we continued the program until I moved out of the area a few years later.

Nobody can tell you what your way to be of service is, but you'll know it when you're in it, and you'll notice what it feels like when you're not in it. When you live your life from a place of service, you're living on your purpose. Some people want their careers to focus on being of service to others. Courtney found a unique way to do this.

Courtney's Story

Courtney was in her early thirties, a top executive in a large marketing firm in the Northeast. She came to me with a desire to rescue horses. She felt called to be of service to animals during the Great Recession, when many people where forced to abandoned their horses due to financial hardship.

Having grown up near stables, with riding as her passion, Courtney had a deep connection to horses. Establishing a rescue farm had been a long-time dream but one she felt was out of reach because she feared letting go of the six-figure income she was earning. Her dream was too important to ignore, so we centered our coaching on rewriting her inherited money belief "You can make money to fund your dream, but you cannot make a living doing your dream."

Courtney's parents were not supportive of her working with horses, and it took almost a year for her to break free from the shame she felt over disappointing them.

During that year, we worked on her vision for a rescue farm. Courtney set up a savings account for the farm and traveled looking for land. Her company got wind of her intention to be of service to animals, and they valued her so much that they offered to set up a satellite office and make a donation so she could establish the rescue farm, while also maintaining a decent income. Her dream started with one horse at a time and became a reality a year later.

SELF-DIRECTION #13: Offer Your Help

There are as many ways to serve others as there are people in this world.

Commit to finding one volunteer activity in your community, and sticking with it for a minimum of a year.

Journal about your volunteer opportunity. How does it feel to help others without receiving any financial compensation for your efforts? What impact does volunteer work have on your relationship with money? What do you enjoy most about what you are doing? What do you want to do more of or less of?

Service is about being in the flow of giving and receiving, so be sure to approach your offerings with an attitude of service. It's also important that you find this experience fulfilling or you will not stick with it.

Repair Your Relationships

When you have money problems, it can be very difficult, if not impossible, to maintain happy, healthy, satisfying relationships. For many people, money problems lead to divorce and separation from family or friends. One of the first signs of a successful money detox is the ability to heal your relationships and live out a shared purpose with your partner. A money detox can literally save your marriage or partnership. Or it can open the door for a new partner to walk in.

The first step is to make amends, as we discussed in the chapter on forgiveness. For some of the people in your life, forgiveness will be enough: you will make amends and then continue on your separate paths in life. But in other cases, forgiveness will be the beginning of repairing and renewing your romantic relationship. Together, you can build a new foundation, one in which you learn to repair small injuries as they occur, and to be honest, open, and accepting of each other so that your relationship heals and grows. Discuss your respective money beliefs and agree never to let differences over money fester without addressing them.

If your money problems have kept you from finding a life partner, after completing the money detox, you may find it is a good time to start dating again. As you do this, be alert for old habits. Make sure when you meet potential partners that they don't represent any of your discarded money patterns. Talk openly with new partners about how you both treat money.

Tara's Story

Many years after we broke up, during my amends process, as I was contacting my exes, I also called Tara. We had played out the most painful money shame together, and it had been a major factor in our break up.

My amends to Tara included:

"I was wrong for expecting you to financially rescue me."

"I was wrong for making you wrong for not financially rescuing me."

"I am sorry that I did not see you, I only focused on seeing your money."

"I was wrong for playing the victim and crying about my financial stress."

"I was wrong for judging you for having more money."

In a full circle moment, Tara hired me to be her money coach! And today we are once again dating.

The Simmons Family Story

The Simmons family consisted of mom, dad, and a teenage boy and girl. I began working with the couple, who blamed each other for all their problems. They were both high earners, in their mid-forties, with $50,000 in credit card debt. They could not hold onto money, and they complained that their kids had been sucking them dry with all their financial needs.

I began meeting with the teenagers separately from the parents to build trust and hear their side of the story. Kids tell the truth! They told me that mom and dad gave them everything they asked for, with no limits. They took what they were given because they wanted their parents to feel good and get along. At the same time, they felt sorry for their parents, who argued all the time, were stressed, and were unhappy in their relationship. The kids felt powerless but wanted to learn about money—something they were not learning about at home or school.

We met once a week after school for about six months. During that time, we covered all the financial basics: credit, bank accounts, budgets, student loans, resumes, interviewing for a job, and family money beliefs. The kids started to bring their friends, and it turned into a small group most days. The kids got jobs and stopped spending so much money on eating out. Once they learned about compounded interest, they ran home to open Roth IRAs.

Imagine all the great things that could happen if we talked about money and shame and inherited money beliefs as a regular subject in school!

8

Thank You, Keith

Although I grew up in Catholicism, spirituality wasn't necessarily my thing. The trauma of my childhood clouded my awareness, causing a delay in my ability to change destructive patterns. My radar was too wrapped around fear, anxiety, and worry to notice much of anything else.

The year before Keith died, a masseuse came to my home. I didn't know he was an intuitive; back then, that would not have been on my radar anyway.

When the masseuse and I were in my bedroom, he said, "Do you know that you have a spirit guide?"

I didn't know what a spirit guide was, and told him so.

"Well, I hesitate to say this because I don't want you to think I'm woo-woo or kooky," he said, "but I am intuitive.

Some things are going on around you that I want to tell you about if you're open to it."

Of course, I was curious.

"Your spirit guide wants you to know that she's here for you; she's supporting you, and you can come to her," he said.

"What are you talking about?" I had no idea what he meant.

He explained that I had a Native American spirit guide, and her name was Rose. "You don't believe me, I know," he said. "So this is what I want you to do. I want you to ask her to give you a sign. Right now. Don't tell me what the sign is, just ask her to give it to you."

It was a hot day, and the door from my bedroom to the beach was open. In my mind, I asked Rose for a cool breeze. I thought I couldn't fake that: the air was so stagnant because of the heat outside.

Out of nowhere, I heard a *whoosh* as a cool breeze brushed right over me. Being me, I tested it a dozen more times. I kept testing it. And testing it. It happened every single time.

After the massage, I went straight to the bookstore to find out about spirit guides. At the time, the only person who had published anything of the sort that I could find was the psychic Sylvia Browne. I bought Sylvia's CD about spirit guides.[1] Back at home, I went to the beach and put the disc

1. Sylvia Browne, *Contacting Your Spirit Guide* (Carlsbad, CA: Hay House, 2015).

into my portable CD player and listened to Sylvia explain how to talk to loved ones from the other side. She said to close your eyes and ask your loved one to come forward, to ask them to bring you a sign to show you that they were there.

The only person I knew at that time who had passed away was my mother's oldest sister. She died of a heart attack in her fifties, and she was a real mother figure to me when she was alive. So I asked Auntie to come forward and bring me a seagull. Specifically, because I was on the beach, I asked her to bring a seagull to my blanket. My eyes were closed, and suddenly I heard *bwaaak!* I opened my eyes, and there was a seagull sitting on the blanket. I immediately burst into tears; it was such a profound experience.

Until that moment, I did not know there was anybody in my corner. I thought I'd been going it alone, at least on the most fundamental level. It never occurred to me before that experience that I could be assisted by my deceased loved ones or by God. My soul got it that day on the beach. It opened my mind in a way that it had never been open before. Despite my years of Catholic schooling, it wasn't until that day that it hit me: if these people were there in spirit, and they were accessible, then maybe that meant I could commune with God, as well.

I went back home and pulled out all the books I had read over the years about spirituality—books I had read but never quite understood. I realized that my mind had been blocked by fear, worry, anxiety, and so many other unfounded things.

Had I not had that experience with the masseuse, I'm not sure I would have been prepared to understand what happened after Keith died.

Almost immediately after he passed, he started coming to me at 3:33 a.m. every morning. I would be sound asleep, and his presence would shake me awake. I had a witness: my Dalmatian, Lucy. After Keith's death, she took it upon herself to sleep directly on the bed with me. When Keith would visit, she would jump up on all fours and growl like crazy.

Several months after Keith died, I received a forwarded email from my aunt Patricia, my mom's other sister. The email was from her friend Deborah, who was a psychic medium:

> Patricia, I'm sorry to hear about your nephew. I heard he passed away. Could you give me his name? There's a spirit guide hanging out with me, and he is such a pest. He is so persistent! I can see Gloria. [My mother and Aunt Patricia's sister] The only name I keep getting is Thomas. I'm taking notes and recording and writing everything down. I'll keep you posted. Deborah

I was shocked to receive this email. I emailed Deborah and explained that Keith had been visiting me every morning at

3:33 a.m., and asked if I could talk to her. I hadn't discussed with anyone what had been happening to me, so I was grateful to find someone who understood and might be able to help.

We had a phone call, and she offered to channel Keith for me.

Our conversations continued for a year, both by phone and in person. Deborah happened to live in Westford, near the ballpark where Keith had some of his best childhood memories. She told me Keith would often come to her in that park.

On October 17, 2007, I went to Westford to join my brother James, some of our cousins, our aunt, our uncle, and Deborah to sprinkle Keith's ashes. Keith was with us in spirit, and we put his ashes where he asked us to, through Deborah. He wanted us to know at that moment, "Carry on with happy memories and the feeling of celebration in your hearts. I do."

Keith's experience in the human world had obviously been a difficult one, as everyone who knew him had been aware. He had struggled with addiction from a young age, and he had intense highs and lows in behavior. Deborah told me in one of our early calls that Keith said, "This is how I feel right now: 'Perfect in beauty, God shines forth'"(Psalm 50.2).

I wondered, *Where is he? How did he go from feeling so crazy and in the place of wanting to commit murder to ultimately killing himself?* I mean, this was within a couple of months of his death, yet he sounded so much at peace. My curiosity had me asking questions like, *Where are you? What are you doing over there? What is this place?*

During our channeling sessions, I gained a tremendous amount of knowledge about life, and the soul's journey and purpose. In his afterlife, Keith was nothing like what I had experienced with him during life. He had been addicted for so long while alive that I had unknowingly lost touch with the real Keith I'd known many years before his death. Now he told me he was finally free of his self-imposed suffering. He wanted to talk about everything he had held inside during his life. He bubbled over with all his thoughts and feelings about all those years of shame and repression. He explained why he chose the path to end his life.

Keith also told me more about his relationship with his wife. Contrary to what my family believed, she hadn't killed him. He took his own life, but it was a volatile "fuck you" to Karen. He said he was so addicted that he'd lost his mind toward the end of his life.

Deborah was careful to ask me how much of the truth I wanted to know. I wondered if the truth was going to help me, and if would I be able to use it for good. She said yes, because I was going to write a book. Only then did she disclose Keith's admission that he probably would have committed a murder-suicide but had instead killed himself.

I was crushed to learn the absolute depth of my brother's

dire straits. How did I not understand what he was going through? How did I not see how low he had sunk? In my mind, I flashed back to our last time together, where during that fateful meeting at Starbucks, I'd money shamed him for his inability to manage money. I recalled my apparent futility in working with him and his wife on their finances that day. If only I'd known then that they were long, long past the place where fixing their finances would have solved anything. They needed an intervention of a significant kind. The channeling helped me realize that finances were not their problem, but a major symptom of a much graver situation.

Through our talks in his afterlife, Keith did his best to assuage my pain. One thing he said that helped tremendously was "Suicide doesn't get you out of doing your soul's work." He said you might as well stay on Earth because you could enjoy chocolate and eat pizza; you could smell the flowers; you could swim in the ocean with your dog; and you could hug your mom. He praised all the work I did. "I'm so proud of you because you've done so much in your life with all the therapy and the AA meetings and working the 12 steps. Just keep doing that."

Keith told me a lot about the afterlife, and how he now worked with soldiers who had committed suicide and wouldn't let themselves leave the human realm. He said they would stick around in spirit and then get stuck in different domains. Many times, they tried to stay close to their families instead of moving on to do their own work. He helped them begin their soul's work and get to the next level.

He shared with me a lot of personal information he wanted our mother and his kids to know. He asked me to have a necklace made for his daughter. He showed me a spiral that looked like an upside-down "e," and said, "I want you to think of me in that symbol. That's love, and it's always continuing. It doesn't matter if I'm here or if I'm there, love continues always. I'm always going to be here, just a thought away." I had the necklace made with that upside-down "e," for Marie, as he'd asked, and transcribed on the back, "Love continues. I'm always with you." I gave that to her per Keith's instructions. He was very adamant that love is constant and always continues, even after death.

We would check in periodically through the medium. In the sixth year after his passing, Keith said he had gotten through all of his soul contracts and had a new understanding of responsibility. He explained that a soul contract is a sacred agreement that your soul makes in order to advance its growth while in this lifetime. Your soul agrees to the kinds of karmic lessons you'll learn, experiences you'll have, and circumstances you'll find yourself in during this lifetime.

"I thought I could get out of my contracts," he said. "I was wrong."

That was powerful to hear. I see a lot of people in my

coaching practice who are on the verge of suicide. They don't often admit to me that they're suicidal, but I know it because I've been there and I know what it looks like. My intuition now is keen. When they come in, and I see that they're suicidal, I carefully ask, "You got a plan?" As I did with Nelson, and like Nelson, they always know what I'm talking about.

I tell them my brother's story. I tell them my brother had been very clear when he told me that you don't get out of doing your work. He said you might as well stay here and have more fun. If you check out early, you're going to have to pay for it in some other way.

I trust that every single person who walks through my door needs to be in my office. I know it before they do, because they wouldn't be coming to me if they didn't have all the same sorts of problems I have had. I trust God sincerely in that way. I also believe in Keith and his work on the other side.

His words changed my heart. I don't know if I would have gotten to where I am today without his death. The entire experience catapulted me through layer after layer of spiritual growth. I could feel his love when I thought of him, and that was something I'd never experienced before. I hadn't even known that something like that was possible. I came to understand that I could connect with Keith just by thinking of him, that his love was all around me and he was only a thought away.

Deborah said Keith was surrounded by spirit animals. She said, "They're from the spirit world, so they are different from what you'd see if you went into the woods." She wanted to know if he was a veterinarian or worked with animals. I said no, but he hunted, so he spent a lot of time in the woods. He went to his tree stand every day and drank himself into a coma because that's where he found peace. He felt the closest to God when he was out in nature. He told me nature is where you can go to experience joy on Earth. Nature is where you can find the feeling he was having over there. He told me to sit on the beach and let that feeling flow. It was surreal to see him as a teacher in the afterlife, as it was unlike how he had been in life.

The essence of what he showed me was that we can be riddled with mental addiction and still be connected to God. We still have that source. It doesn't get taken from us, no matter what we do on Earth. We all can recover. We all have the same shot, no matter what we come in with, because we all can tap into God or spirit or the universe or whatever you want to call it. What was so profound about his death was that he was liberated from his suffering.

The primary thing Keith wanted to make sure I heard was "Love continues." What I interpreted that to mean was that love is the key to everything. Love is what allowed me to do the deep work and move to a place of deeper self-examination and look closely at forgiveness. Knowing love continues moved me into a place of forgiving myself and others in a bigger way. Keith was the catalyst for this shift. Every time I talked to him, that was the message I received. He instructed me to keep carrying that message forward, and I do.

The time came when I needed to let go, and Keith had to let go of me. Once I got connected with him, I couldn't sleep. I was feeling run down, and I was kind of sick. It was taking a lot out of me to maintain the afterlife connection with Keith. But it was tough to give him up because, contrary to how we had been during the last ten years of his life, we had developed a close relationship in his afterlife. Hanging with Keith felt like I was in a cocoon with him, safe and secure. There was no fear. There was no judgment. There was only a healthy relationship with a beautiful exchange of information.

Along came the day when I had to say to him, "Keith, you've gotta go to the next thing." That's when I felt the grief of losing him in an entirely different way. The new Keith I'd come to know and love had to leave. Before leaving, he assured me again that he was just a thought away. He said he would always be around. I can call him in whenever I want. I no longer need a medium because I can talk to him openly. I believe that we will always be together, forever.

My brother Keith's legacy lives on in you and me through sharing our stories. Our legacy is not defined by our net worth but by how many lives we touch along the way.

Thank you for taking this walk through a money detox with me. Please carry this revolution forward and share your money story. Be the one to break the cycle.

About the Author

Tammy Lally is a Certified Money Coach, TEDx Speaker, and author of *Money Detox*. She helps others master their finances by first conquering their emotions around money, then by creating a comprehensive financial plan. She has seventeen years of experience in the financial industry and twenty-seven years of study in the fields of psychology, addiction, recovery, and spirituality. Her teachers include Gurumayi Chidvilasananda, Marianne Williamson, Brene Brown, Byron Katie, Pia Mellody, and Edwene Gaines. She brings a unique, multifaceted consciousness to her coaching practice, offering a compassionate approach to help clients heal their relationship with money and achieve powerful, and in many cases, life-altering results in their financial and emotional lives.

Tammy has created and designed the **Money Detox**, a seven-part process that allows anyone to achieve financial freedom and joy. "After seventeen years in the financial industry, I know a 'financial plan' is not enough to help those looking for the path to financial freedom and to escape the loop of money shame. Money issues and shame continue to be a major life struggle for millions of people, and I have dedicated my life to assisting them," she says.

Today Tammy works with clients to discover, question, and own their often-hidden money beliefs and behaviors, as well as identify the impact these beliefs can have on their financial, social, emotional, and spiritual well-being. Through a distinctive blend of acquired knowledge, experience, and the sharing of her money shame healing story, Tammy exposes the truth about how to change what keeps people broken—and broke—in their relationship with money.

Tammy currently lives in Maitland Florida, with Bella, her golden retriever. She works with clients in person, by phone, or via Skype.

Contact:

Tammy Lally
The Money Coach
  Certified Money Coach (CMC)®
Website: tammylally.com
Email: money@tammylally.com
Skype: TammyLally1

Follow Me!
Facebook: www.facebook.com/heartofmoney
LinkedIn: www.linkedin.com/in/tammylally
Twitter: twitter.com/tammylally

Notes

CPSIA information can be obtained
at www.ICGtesting.com
Printed in the USA
FFHW010155131218
49849273-54405FF